CW00542217

- A MEMOIR -

THE DAY MY MOTHER NEVER CAME HOME

REGINALD L. REED JR.

The Day My Mother Never Came Home

Copyright © 2023 by Reginald L. Reed Jr.

All rights reserved. No part of this book may be reproduced or used in any manner without the prior written permission of the copyright owner, except for the use of brief quotations in a book review.

Additional works cited:

Amso, Dima. "When Do Children Start Making Long-Term Memories?" January 1, 2017. https://scientificamerican.com/article/when-do-children-start-making-long-term-memories/

Van der Kolk, Bessel A. 2014. *The Body Keeps the Score*. Penguin Random House, LLC.

Arledge, H.L. 2019. *Bayou Justice*. Draft2Digital

Dr. Thema Bryant-Davis and Sigrid Ellis quotes obtained via the World Wide Web.

Isaiah 59:10—The Holy Bible.

Consulting by Freedom Press.

Editing by Stacey Barbin Higgins.

Cover design and interior typeset by twolineSTUDIO.

ISBN: 979-8-9897111-1-6 (paperback)
    979-8-9897111-0-9 (hardback)

TABLE OF CONTENTS

PART III: THE WAITING

PART IV: THE TRIAL

On August 23, 1987, the body of Selonia Reed, 26, was found partially clothed in the passenger seat of her blue 1986 Chevrolet Sprint in an empty parking lot in Hammond, Louisiana. She had sustained blunt force trauma to her head and face, her upper body suffering more than a dozen stab wounds. She had also been sexually violated with an umbrella.

Officials noted no defensive injuries or wounds, and her death was ruled a homicide.

Selonia Reed is my mother.

I was six at the time.

PREFACE

I begin this book with a simple confession: what you are about to read is extremely hard for me to articulate. It is important to understand that even now, as I write these words, I am at the beginning of this journey—of unraveling it all. I will often speak to you of my wounds, and the accompanying pain, trauma, and suffering. My wound is the giant hole in my heart left by the loss of my mother.

I did not get to grow up with and know my mother in the traditional sense, sharing experiences and memories in the way that a typical grown man would. We did not have those years of creating memories together. The trauma of her loss and my subsequent grieving are intangible and abstract. I cannot point to the pain as I could a broken arm or leg and say, "There. That is exactly where the break is. That is where it hurts." I cannot explain away my suffering with a diagnosis; something life-altering or terminal like cancer. I feel the grief deep in my bones, an ever-present ache that is more real than anything I have ever known.

It is hard for me to wrap my mind around everything, let alone explain it to others. It feels as if I am grieving a collection of shadows and ghosts, things I never really knew well enough to be able to feel the weight of their loss—and yet, I do. Perhaps this can be explained by science; the unbreakable bond between a mother and child due to the DNA we share. The eternal connection between us formed because I was part of her, and she will always be a part of me. Surely there is some fancy explanation for the immense void that I feel. Science or not, the ache is prodigious. It is emotional, and visceral. My physical body, heart, and mind all bear the longing and loss in equal measure. The persistent yearning for my mother has developed in layers; different when I was six than it was at nine, fifteen, and twenty. It is exponentially different today, as a man of forty. I still feel it in all the old ways; but, as a grown man and father, I have added new layers of pain, each one equally torturous.

The cumulation of decades of emotional trauma has formed a scab, making peeling the trauma back layer by layer the hardest and most heart-wrenching work I will ever do. The facts are simple, really. I am a man who longs for his mother. I believe most people can sympathize with this basic need, and yet my story is much more than this. My story is immensely complex. Perhaps you too have known heartbreak and suffering and can understand how difficult healing can be. Although words seem to fall so incredibly short of the nuances and intricacies of my thoughts, feelings, and emotions, I invite you into my story—I trust you with my story—and I hope you will see and hear my heart and look beyond my limitations.

INTRODUCTION

This is my story.

I have chosen to tell it now because I have experienced much, endured much—I have lived a lot of life. But all I have suffered and lost means nothing unless by telling my truths, my story can benefit others. I can no longer contain the pain within myself. The weight of it has become too much for one man to bear. While my narrative may not be perfectly written, or even eloquently articulated, and I struggle at times to describe what and how I feel, I am in the rawest sense simply a man with a story that must be told. And having declared it, may it set me free.

My aspiration is that as you read these pages, my story gives you strength. I hope that you will recognize within these chapters and paragraphs pieces of your own story; perhaps some that you can no longer bear witness to alone. I desire that you find the will to begin your own journey of healing and break through whatever holds you hostage or weighs you down. I want you to feel the freedom that is possible in letting go.

While writing this book I discovered some important truths about myself, as well as the processes of survival and healing. One such truth is having compassionate witnesses who are actively engaged in our lives is vital to our survival. Compassionate witnesses are individuals who listen without judgment, and who allow us to voice the words that have been swirling around in

our minds, desperately wanting to come out. There is great healing in this exchange. Compassionate witnesses can be trusted
friends, family members, or individuals who have been through
similar experiences if they can simply listen to your stories without the need to *fix it*.

Sadly, I fear that listening has become a lost art. We do not
like to see people in pain, especially when it is someone that we
love. We want to hurry up and fix it, then file it away in a neat
little box. But that's not how listening works. Much like me,
people just need to voice their truth and find an understanding
ear on the other end. Feeling the pain and speaking the truth
of it are both part of the healing process. We don't need more
fixers in the world; we need more *listeners*. We need people who
are comfortable sitting beside us in the messy middle, quietly
listening and allowing us to work through all the things that we
are feeling inside...

Because the truth is, we don't actually need *fixing*.

I encourage you to find a compassionate witness and ask
them to walk a while with you on your journey. I hope that in
turn, you will be such to others. You may find great healing in
the simplicity of sitting quietly beside another person, bearing
witness to their pain for those brief moments, and saying *I know,
me too*. It's so simple, and yet revolutionary—it could change the
world.

There are no right or wrong ways to heal. It is different for
every individual and what works for me won't work for everyone. I often think of the healing process as the *messy middle*. It's
like being stuck in the mud on a deserted dirt road on a cold and

rainy night. The car tires spin fruitlessly, slinging red mud onto the windows so fast and thick that you are unable to see the road through the muck. You're cold, alone, and scared. You're pissed off, and ready to give up. As the tires dig trenches deeper and deeper, you begin to realize that you only have two choices: Sit here alone and freeze to death in the cold, wet darkness, or call for help.

Healing is far from neat or tidy; in fact, it's downright messy. It is important to remember that there are no *right* or *wrong* ways to heal. Healing is not a linear process, and there are no straight lines to follow. The healing process is different for each person, but I promise you it is worth every ounce of effort and every minute spent. As you read my story, I hope that you will be reminded of and experience immense gratitude for the people, relationships, and many loves in your life. May you take time to look at them in new ways, seeing their unique beauty, love, and value in your life and the lives of others. In the end, nothing else will matter except the people that we love and the relationships that we have nurtured along the way. Nothing is more important than the love we give to others and the love we allow ourselves to receive. When the time comes to look back on your journey, everything else will fade in comparison.

It has taken me a very long time to arrive at this place. I was uncertain that this book would ever get written, let alone shared. I never thought I would have the courage to deeply reflect on my life—the good and the bad—and write it down for the world to read. I am ready now. These stories have been bouncing around in the recesses of my mind for three decades, and it is time for them to emerge.

My story is full of sadness, heartache, unresolved traumas, and deep wounds that still need attention. The human experience is hard, and often full of pain and suffering. None of us is exempt from the hardships of this life, and while mine have been almost unbearable at times, there has also been boundless joy, unconditional love, abundant success, and great triumph. The pages of my story are bound in immense suffering, but each sentence and line weaves a tale of healing, redemption, and hope.

Look for hope. Do not dwell on the sad parts; instead, search for the sources of joy that can arise from any experience—good or bad—if we only allow it. When you turn the last page of this book and reflect upon the entirety of my story—and your own story—my greatest wish is that you meditate on the fragility of life and the pain of the human experience, recalling the formidable strength and fierce resilience of the human spirit and its capacity to love, endure, and at last triumph over even the most horrific experiences. Trust me. I am proof.

Above all, I wish for you to discover your *own* worth and your immeasurable value. Despite what you have walked through, and all the pain and suffering you have survived or are currently enduring, I hope you will open your eyes to the boundless strength and resilience that you possess. May you begin to realize your unique gifts and accept that you are the only person who can truly tell your story—and that story is worth telling.

I invite you to tell your story. The world needs your words, even the messy ones—especially the messy ones. The world needs more truth-tellers and seekers of healing and wholeness. One life at a time; examined, healed, and restored. I believe this is how we truly change the world.

Let my life and my words serve as an invitation to you, a way of permitting you to step into your own story. Take time to reflect deeply on all that you have experienced and survived—everything that has made you who you are today—and write it down as a map to freedom. It is so worth it. Voicing your pain will be one of the most difficult things that you ever do; it will also be one of the most rewarding experiences of your life. There is so much healing on the other side of your pain—I promise.

I have been through much, and I have endured more than many. But, through everything, I have known true and boundless love and experienced the greatest heights of joy. I have been cared for and adored, encouraged, and lifted by the people in my life; I hope I have done the same for them. I am strong and capable, and I am uniquely me. I accept all that I have been through and everything that I have survived and seek now the great lessons it will teach me. Life can be so frightfully hard, even brutal at times; but it is still so beautiful, even more so than on the darkest night. For as it has been said, we must be completely engulfed by the darkness to fully see the brilliance of the light.

Thank you for walking with me on this journey; and for being my compassionate witness. Thank you for listening to my words and shouldering some of my burdens for a bit.

I am forever grateful.

And above all else, I have great hope.

Endless hope.

PART ONE

THE BEFORE

THE BEGINNING

I t makes sense—at least in my mind—that I begin writing my story now, before the trial. I want to remember my life with my father in it, fully present. I want to reflect on the time we spent together; growing up, making our way the best we knew how, and processing our suffering side by side after losing the greatest love of our lives. I want to recall every detail from a life interrupted and forever marked by trauma. I also want to look back and reflect on how all along my life was preparing me for this moment.

I would not wish this kind of pain and suffering on anyone, but I am finally at a place in my life where I am eager and ready to get down to the business of living a full and abundant life. I know I cannot get there without first going backward. It has been said that we should not slam the door in fear when pain comes knocking. We should invite it in, ask it to take a seat and tell it not to leave until we have discovered all that we need to learn. I heard the knock, and at last, I have answered the door. I sit here with the pain, learning, growing, finding my voice, and healing. The more time that I spend commiserating with my pain, the more I realize that this will be a lifelong endeavor.

I am a man who holds my cards extremely close to my chest; however, I have decided that this book will be different. It *must* be different. Everything must be sorted through and shared because I cannot continue as I have been. It won't be pretty, no bows or ribbons. It will be raw, unsophisticated, and unrefined—but it will be real.

This is my story. My truth. There is a clear beginning but lacks the traditional middle or end, like most people's stories. My life doesn't flow in this way; it never has. The stories I will share have been bouncing around in my heart and mind for more than three decades, waiting for exactly the right time to emerge.

Now is the time.

Within these pages you will find the memories of a six-year-old boy whose mother was murdered; a ten-year-old boy entering his teen years with all of the awkwardness and confusion of a typical adolescent; a fifteen-year-old young man searching for his place in the world without the guidance and encouragement of his mother; and a 39-year-old man living amid the preset day trauma as his father—his best friend—awaits trial for the murder.

His wife's murder.

My mother's murder.

So much of my life feels like dots that never connect. It becomes frustrating at times and can feel overwhelming and unfair. My mother was stolen from me, and now I must consider the possibility of my father being ripped from my life as well. The thought of losing both mother and father feels like my heart has stopped beating, and I wait for my lungs to remind me that I must *breathe*. I am paralyzed, caught in the middle of a terrible nightmare that never ends.

To make sense of everything, I compartmentalize my life into three distinct parts: Part One is my life as a boy and a young man. Part Two is my life now. Part Three is yet to come. Part three is my father's murder trial, the outcome to be decided upon in a courtroom by twelve of his peers. Part three is my future and my father's future. As I begin writing, Part Three is still very much a mystery, and completely unknown. I can only pray for the best possible outcome for me, my father, and my family. I pray that justice prevails, and the truth is revealed. The fact that I have zero control over the outcome is an impossibly hard reality to sit with. Like much of my life, I feel that in this instance I am once again simply collateral damage. My mother is dead, and my father may go to prison for life, and I will be left alone to carry on.

I have played out every possible scenario in my mind, and regardless of how I spin it, there is no perfect outcome. If my father is found innocent—as I believe him to be with all my heart—we will all still be left with the question of who took her life. My mother will have no justice. If my father is convicted, my heart will shatter once again. If I learn things about my father that I never knew or thought him capable of, I will have to some-how make peace with the man I think I know versus the man he is. The heaviness of that reality is unbearable and often feels like too much for one person to carry. The hard truth is that nothing will bring my mother back; she is gone forever, and I will never know her. The depth of sadness I feel over her loss is indescribable.

A friend recently asked me how I see my life when I sit qui-etly and ponder all that I have been through. They expressed— as many people do—that they could not understand how I had endured so much and had still been able to lead a successful life. When I took the time to meditate quietly on this, a specific feeling emerged: When I think about my life there is a definitive split. There is the *before*, and there is *now*.

Before is my life as a boy and a young man trying to figure out life, school, and relationships with all my grief and feelings surrounding my mother's death.

Before is Hammond, Louisiana.

Before is my little childhood home on Apple Street.

Before is me and my father surviving after the worst possible trauma.

Now is my life after the before. Now is today—three decades years later. Now is marriage to my wife and the beginning of fatherhood with our first-born son. Now is a successful career in pharmaceutical sales. Now is San Antonio, Texas, and owning my first home. Now is making peace with the reality that I endured actual childhood trauma and that it has informed every part of my life. Now is waiting for the trial to come, and wondering what the next part of my life will be like.

The parts of my life don't overlap in my mind or thoughts; in fact, they are distinctly separate. I *had* to separate them in order to move past the pain of my childhood loss and move forward with my life. I had to decide which world I would live in because I could not exist with one foot in each space. With that decision, I leaped into the now. I had to. I could no longer live solely in the past. That is not to say I no longer think about my mother, or that I have completely shut myself off from everything that occurred. Things are not that black and white. It is a complicated yet conscious decision that I make every single day—*Live in the NOW*.

We all know that suffering and loss can change people, even more so if endured as a child who cannot fully understand what has occurred. I often wonder if doctors and mental health professionals are capable of fully understanding the damage inflicted upon the psyche of a six-year-old boy who suddenly loses his mother to violence unless they have lived through it. In my personal life, I have not encountered a single individual who shares my specific trauma—my unique story. Perhaps this person does not exist. Perhaps there is not a single person in the world who can fully understand the depth and complexity of my specific suffering. This thought process can be intensely lonely and isolating, and I suppose part of making the decision to write this book was to search for others who could understand my pain. I hope that as people read the story of my life, I will feel some understanding and compassion in the sharing. I hope that as you read, you too, will find some understanding and compassion for *your* specific wounds.

The full emotional impact of my mother's death is unknown. Childhood trauma is unique and complex, and its long-term effects are unlike other types of trauma. Childhood trauma does not leave behind gaping wounds that one can physically see and mend, such as a broken arm or leg. The damage is locked inside, hidden, covered up by the passage of time and its attempt to heal, or at the very least, conceal. The wounds never fully heal, though. They are too deep and too buried to ever recover completely. Only now am I beginning to expose my wounds to the light. It is painful and brutally difficult because the truth is, they never *truly* heal. Exposure is like experiencing the first cut all over again.

It is necessary, though, and it is time.

I no longer want to feel this weight—I want to be free. I want to help others learn how to be free, to teach them how to walk through their tragedies and come out the other side stronger. I want my pain to mean something and have a purpose. I need every bit of it to *matter*. I believe that sharing my pain can help others heal, and in turn, give me the clarity that I so desire. Without this transparency, my suffering will remain buried deep inside, a festering wound that never heals. I need to uncover everything and transform every piece of it, or I will slowly disappear under the weight. I believe that helping others will give my pain meaning and purpose—and I need it to have a purpose.

But first, I must start with myself.

I have recently become a father to a beautiful baby boy named Lathan, the middle name of both my father and myself. The experience of becoming a father—especially to a son—has changed me. I no longer live only for myself; I am living for *him*. I still very much live life on the surface, skimming along in survival mode; but I recognize that this is not fair to him, my wife, or our little family, and I want to change. I don't make a conscious decision to exist on this plane; it is the coping mechanism of deep childhood trauma. Our mental and physical bodies are hardwired to fight, and I fought as well. I had two choices after my mother was killed: Survive and thrive, or sink and drown, dragged down by the weight of my grief. I chose to survive and have spent the past three decades fighting—overcoming.

I am tired.

No, that isn't entirely true. I am *exhausted*.

Our bodies keep score even if our minds will not allow us to visit the places of pain and sorrow buried deep within. The body reaches a point at which it can no longer function in its current state. For many, this manifests as physical symptoms such as depression, anxiety, insomnia, and other ailments. The body sends out rescue flares, begging for attention—screaming for help. For me, there are very few physical symptoms, at least at this point. My heart races sometimes, perhaps it is a bit of anxiety, or something as simple as heartburn. It is hard to know for sure when you have lived in this state for so long. My most troublesome symptom is emotional, much harder to identify and remedy because it is internal and woven into every aspect of my life. I cannot separate myself from it. I know it is not *who* I am and that it does not define me, but it still very much dictates my life and relationships.

My past has stolen my ability to be fully present in my life and with the people I love. It has created a fierce independence within me. I carry the weight of the world on my shoulders because it is easier to do it myself than to trust others to help me carry it. To put one's trust in others is unpredictable, and scary. What if they don't come through for me? At least I know I can trust myself and that I can and will get shit done. I always have, even as a young boy. Rather than allowing people to help and carry some of my great weight, I just keep grinding along, doing what I do, moving forward one step at a time.

I have learned that this is common in survivors of childhood trauma, especially when it involves the loss of a parent. It is a coping mechanism that elicits a sense of safety and protection. For example, if I don't allow myself to *feel* too much, or share pieces of myself with another person, I will never get hurt. If I don't allow myself to be fully engaged in my life, I will never feel regret or disappointment. If I don't love deeply and fully, I will never feel loss. This all seems like a very good plan, but it is a screen, a false sense of security and safety. I have become imprisoned by the walls that I have built around myself, and I fear that nothing can get in. I am incapable of feeling deeply or being fully present for anyone or anything in my life. I can't immerse myself in fatherhood or give my complete self to my marriage because I am deeply afraid; afraid of loss or of being abandoned, I suppose. It is this fear and the mechanisms that I have established to cope with it which are stealing the joy from my life and isolating the best parts of me from the people that I love the most. It is keeping me from fully living.

This is not to say that I have no joy in my life. Quite the contrary. I absolutely do find happiness in many things and appreciate that my life is full of blessings. I have a beautiful wife and a healthy son, a very successful career, and a beautiful home in a city that I love. However, I am learning that happiness is not *joy*. Happiness and joy are two very different emotions. Happiness is fleeting and circumstantial; a momentary feeling of euphoria brought on by a surge of endorphins. If all goes well in my life, I am happy. If my son smiles at me, I am happy. Joy, on the other hand, is an unconditional peace that exists *despite* a person's circumstances. It is deep peace and contentment.

I long to feel joy. I long to just *be*. I want a healthy emotional life that allows me to be the best version of myself in every aspect of my life. I want to live wide awake, in tune with my feelings as they occur, and able to process and integrate them into my life in healthy ways. I want to be fully present as a man, husband, son, friend, and most importantly, a father. I do not yet know if growing up without a mother by my side will influence my parenting, or if my inability to connect deeply will affect my marriage. Will I be able to fully connect with my son? I often struggle to give what I did not receive—the love of a mother—so I will need to fight harder for a fulfilling marriage and a meaningful relationship with my children.

I must learn to set aside my feelings of longing and loss in order to provide the emotional connections that were taken from me. This will take time, patience, and hard work; unlearning decades of old thought patterns and behaviors and re-learning new ways of living, being present, trusting even when it feels risky, and fully connecting with the people around me, especially my little family. There is absolutely no replacement for a mother's love. I don't truly understand the sweeping effects this must have had on my life; however, I am beginning to see the impacts of my mother's absence; they are vast, deep, wide, and endless. Her loss has affected every aspect of my life thus far and will surely affect my marriage and parenting. My relationship with my wife and how I raise my son will be completely different than that of a husband and father who has known the deep and unconditional love of a mother.

I have no reference point for the kind of love and encouragement a mother gives. That part of my heart is empty. Will I be a good husband? Will my wife know how much I love her, even when it is hard for me to show? Will I be a good father? Will I be good enough for my son? Will I overcompensate and be a smothering force in his life? I imagine I will ask these questions of myself time and time again throughout my life. I don't know if I will ever be completely confident in marriage or parenting. I long for the voice of my mother encouraging my efforts. I long to hear the simple affirmations I am sure she would readily offer, such as "You're doing a good job, son."

My heart sinks a bit as I type these simple words: *You're doing a good job, son*. They elicit such a deep yearning to be seen and known by the one person who can never speak them. My heart aches. There is no healing.

It is crazy how losing her affects every layer and season of my life in different and ever-evolving ways. It never goes away. Never. Platitudes like *time heals all wounds* must have been coined by someone who had never walked through the valley of the shadow of death because the anguish never goes away. Time may take away some of the sting, but it does nothing to heal. Time simply puts distance between you and the event. Time is a band-aid covering some of the wound, but it has not and will never heal my deep pain.

Trauma is tricky. There are some days that I do not think about my mother, days when I am busy living my life. There are also days when she is at the forefront of my thoughts, like a shadow I cannot quite grasp, a heavy presence so painfully out of reach. The latter is the standard of my existence. My mother lives vividly in my thoughts and mind on these days.

I find it hard to reconcile the fact that I never *really* knew her and that all the wonderful and loving memories I could have had were ripped away and stolen on the day she never came home.

MEMORIES

I get asked all the time about the day my mother never came home. It began with the police, my family, and eventually everyone around me.

What could have happened to your mother?

Why did she not come home?

What do you think happened?

The questions that began immediately after her death are the same ones I am asked today, three decades later. It can be relentless at times, especially now as we await the trial. It is as if people expect me to have some sort of crystal ball, or photographic memory, holding the key to all the answers that will solve the case. They look to satisfy their curiosities with these questions, and I've got nothing to offer. I don't owe them or anyone else anything. Their questions raise additional levels of frustration because it is as if I *should* know, that the answers should be within my grasp, and yet, are not.

Memory and memories are defined in two ways: 1. The faculty by which the mind stores and remembers information; and 2. Something remembered from the past; a recollection. I do not hold the stored information, memories, remembrances, or recollections from that part of my past; at least nothing that would unlock any single part of the mystery of my mother's death. I was simply a six-year-old boy living a normal, ordinary day. There was nothing special, different, or unique about it, and I had no reason to capture and preserve each second in my memory. Six-year-old boys don't spend their days recording every moment in case it might be their last with the ones they love. I certainly didn't take mental pictures of every single instant; although now, I wish I had.

I wish I had recorded every second of the last day with my mother. I wish I had taken in every word that she spoke, every touch, and every glance that she gave me. I wish I had studied her face, feeling each curve and feature with my tiny hands; the beauty of her cheeks and the smooth, dark skin leading down to a few smile lines that had begun forming around her mouth. I wish I had held her beautiful brown face in my hands and stared into her eyes, memorizing every speck of their almond color and the way they lit up when she smiled, especially when she was smiling at *me*. I want to rewind the tape, go back, and relive this day. I want to hear my mother's voice, the cadence of her speech, and the slight southern drawl that lent a tenderness to her tone.

I am certain that my mother spoke words of love over me before she left our house on that fateful, horrible night. I know without a doubt that she wrapped me close, hugging my small body and kissing my little boy cheeks and forehead. In my mind, I imagine that she tickled me a bit and told me to *have fun, but don't stay up too late*, the things a loving mother would do and say to her only son. The problem is, I just can't remember it. There is a massive concrete wall between me and my memories of this day. I know that everything I yearn for is on the other side, just out of my reach. Why can't I remember? I beg my psyche to give me something—anything.

I want to remember the interactions between my mother and father that day; the way they made breakfast together in the kitchen, the inside jokes and belly laughs shared, the loving glances and connection of a young couple who had worked hard at making a beautiful life together. In my mind I see them there, a young couple very much in love, despite their challenges and committed to me with all their hearts. If only I had memorized this love and hidden it away, far within myself where I could access it at will and feel it surrounding me. I know it was there because it was made clear through the recollections of others. I have been told that I was the apple of my mother's eye, her most precious pride and joy, and that she beamed when she looked at me, and I at her. But those memories are not mine; they do not belong to me. To me, their stories are like looking at a photograph and allowing it to take you back to a moment and place captured in time when you yourself have no real recollection of the experience.

It is like trying to catch a shadow.

This is my story and my experience, but I can only borrow memories from photos or the recollections of other people. But that is the problem: I am just *borrowing*. These memories are not mine to keep, and I must eventually return them to whom they belong. They have no permanent home in my mind. I was not old enough to retain memories of my own, or maybe the trauma of losing her caused me to lock them away someplace remote and unreachable within my mind.

Memory is unique and fascinating in that a specific memory is essentially a unit of experience, and every experience shapes the brain in meaningful ways. Specific memories and experiences may be forgotten, but because those memories form the fabric of our identities, knowledge, and experiences, they are never truly or completely gone. (Amso, Dima 2017)

She doesn't visit me in my dreams. I know she's in there somewhere, but I just don't know how to find her. If only I had been a few years older I am certain that I would have stored enough memories of her that we could meet in my dreams, building a life all our own in those precious sleeping hours, untainted by grief and devoid of trauma.

If only.

It is not memories that haunt me, but their complete absence. Why can't I remember the good parts of that day, before she left and never came home? I would give anything to go back to that day. I would study and emblazon every moment in my mind. I would etch her face on my heart and the sound of her voice in my spirit. I want to go back, wrap my body around hers in an everlasting embrace and never let her go. I want another chance to memorize her heartbeat, the rhythmic sound thrumming beneath the warmth of her chest as she pressed against my tiny cheek, her body rising and falling as she took the last breaths I would ever feel her take.

I have so much to say to her. I want to listen intently, hanging on every word she speaks and watching her mouth for each word. I would not take my eyes off of her, not even for a second. If only I could go back to this day, I would take the memories and create a secret place where they could live, sealing them up in a tight box, all for myself. I would never again need to borrow memories from pictures or stories. I would lock my memories up and throw the key into the depths of the ocean, and they would be mine, and only *mine*. She would be mine, *only* mine, and I would be hers.

Together.

Forever.

THE DAY MY MOTHER
NEVER CAME HOME

The day my mother left and never came home began as another ordinary Saturday for our small family. It was a lazy weekend in late August, and no one was rushing to get up and out the door to school or work. My parents allowed me to stay up later on weekends, so I am fairly certain that I would have slept in, waking to the smell of bacon frying in the pan and the sounds of my parents cooking in the kitchen. In my mind we sat in our small kitchen and ate breakfast together, talking about the sorts of things we would like to do that day. My mother likely made pancakes for me, my favorite then, and still today. I see us there, working together to clean up the breakfast dishes, chatting and laughing as my mother instructs me on how to properly wash, rinse, and dry a dish. Once the kitchen was clean my father would say, "Go on now, Lil' Reggie, wash your hands, brush your teeth, and get yourself dressed." My mother would give me a loving pat on the behind as I tried to linger, and then off I would go to get ready for the day.

I am sure that you can imagine this scenario playing out in households across the world. There was absolutely nothing remarkable about this particular morning. Our little family was simply doing the everyday unremarkable things that so easily become routine, like waking up, eating breakfast, enjoying conversation, laughing together, and getting ready for the day. The fact that there were no signs of the impending tragedy bothers me. We had absolutely no reason to treat this morning any differently, so we didn't.

I have been told that we decided to go to the local mall, a decision that was not unusual, or something that I would have locked into my memory. We went to the mall a lot. We headed out around noon, my mother driving us in her car, my dad riding shotgun, and me in the back seat, cattycorner from my mother. The August heat would have been stifling, and in my mind's eye I see my parents rolling down the windows as we drove, the sweet, damp Louisiana breeze washing over my six-year-old face. I see my mother's dark, curly hair shining in the sunlight, ringlets dancing in the wind as my father leaned in, tuning the radio to his favorite station, and then sitting back, relaxing, arm on the windowsill as his fingers tapped time to the music. Tap . . . tap . . . tap . . . I begin to tap my foot in the same cadence, joining him in the perfection of this moment. We are all so happy, and life is full of endless possibilities and wonder. We drive along on this ordinary day, almost floating, without a single care in the world, just another family going to the mall on a perfect Saturday morning.

I imagine that we spent a few hours walking around the mall, window shopping at various stores, or going into some for a closer look. I don't remember my parents buying anything specific, but my father would likely have purchased a new game to play on Nintendo. He knew I loved games, and truth be told, he loved them too. It was a fun pastime that we shared, a way to escape the real world and dive into the imaginary worlds of video games.

I have one very clear memory of my parents buying me a chocolate chip cookie from one of the vendors. You know the ones— you can smell the cookies from a mile away. Even today I swear they pump that smell into the air ducts just hoping a kid will catch a whiff and beg their parents for a cookie. In this instance their strategy worked because my parents bought me a cookie. It was warm, wrapped in parchment, placed in a small bag, and handed to me with a smile. Maybe the reason that my mind held on to *this* memory was because it was not ordinary. Fresh-baked chocolate chip cookies always feel special, and I can imagine their warm deliciousness. As usual, I am sure that I had chocolate around every corner of my mouth, and my mother would have wiped it away while smiling and asking, "Is it good?" to which I would have replied that it was the best chocolate chip cookie in the history of chocolate chip cookies.

It is here that things start to blur: My mind skips and the memory swirls like fog in the rain. I have been told so many stories about this day and I allow myself to imagine the rest, borrowing bits and pieces of other people's memories and combining them with fragments of my own. As a grown man, my mind refuses to allow me to bring specific details to the surface, and I am forced to find solace in what I remember about the routines of our life. We would have eaten lunch when we returned home; perhaps it was just a snack since I had eaten the cookie at the mall. It is also possible that we skipped lunch altogether and had an early dinner since my mother was planning to go out for the evening. Either of these scenarios along with a host of others could be true, and I suppose the details of lunch and dinner don't really matter in the grand scheme of things. I tell myself this now—that the mundane details don't matter—but that isn't true. I want to remember the details. I want to remember every minute detail of each moment of that day.

As day gave way to dusk, I know my mother would have begun getting ready to go out, a fun girl's night with her friend Michelle and a couple of girlfriends from the local bank where she worked. She would have made sure my dad and I were taken care of, well-fed, and happily playing video games together in the living room when she prepared to leave.

Just another typical, unremarkable Saturday night, with nothing out of the ordinary. My mother went out with her friends regularly, especially Michelle. Neither my father nor I had any reason to question who she was going out with, where they were going, or have any reason to worry about when she would come home. As her husband and son, we trusted that when wives and mothers go out, they always come home. She had done this dozens of times and always came home.

Why would this time be any different?

As dusk turned to night, we said our goodbyes, showering her with hugs and kisses—then she was gone.

My mother was gone.

Gone.

Gone forever.

My father and I played Nintendo after she left, laughing, and eating popcorn late into the night. It was Saturday, so there were no strict bedtime rules for me. We played until we both grew tired and drifted off to sleep in the living room. The night hours passed, turning into the early morning as my father and I peacefully slept. Now, knowing the circumstances that transpired that night, I can hardly bear to let my mind think of the horrific torment my mother was enduring as my father and I slept safely in our beds.

I have read all the reports, and I know as much as the authorities do about the details of her death. I cannot allow myself to linger too long on the details, because it is just too much to bear. She did not disappear into the night; snatched up or taken, never to be seen again. She did not make a hasty turn while driving her car, to be struck and killed by the impact of another vehicle. The untimely death of a person never makes sense, and murder by definition is rarely peaceful; but my mother's death was unfathomably brutal, violent, and even sadistic.

My heart knows that she was terrified, experiencing a kind of deep and primal fear that you or I cannot even imagine. My heart knows that she suffered, fighting hard for her life, scratching and clawing, the deep guttural sound of her screams echoing against the dark summer sky. There was no one there to save her. No one deserves to take their last breaths in such fear, terror, and unfathomable pain, desperate thoughts filled with the many loves you will leave behind. I wonder if she thought of me in her final moments. I like to imagine that she did.

This is an awful thing to hope for and even worse to imagine. *I hope she thought of me as she was dying.*
What an incredibly fucked up thought to have.

This is not typical, normal, or ordinary.

I feel deep, visceral pain when I allow myself to imagine my mother in her final moments. There is a deep ache that never goes away at the thought of it, like a deep punch to the gut, and I double over with the intensity. It is a million pounds of bricks sitting squarely on my chest, only allowing me to take in the tiniest sips of air as my heart breaks into a million tiny pieces. If I allow myself, I could suffocate under the immense weight of it. It is that heavy; heavier than anyone can imagine.

Our perfectly unremarkable day ended horrifically. Although the details of the day are hazy, I can say with absolute certainty that this day that began so routinely ordinary was—and will always be—the worst day of my life. No one should end their life in this way. No one should lose their wife and mother in this way, with such disregard and violent brutality. No one.

Especially not *my* mother.

MY MOTHER'S MURDER

If my mother had been in an accident or became ill and passed away, I think I would have made sense of her death over time. Accidents happen, and people get sick; in fact, people die every second of every single day. It is the fact that another human being made the conscious decision to end my young mother's life in such an inhumane and ruthless way that I cannot now and will never be able to make sense of.

The facts of my mother's murder are unthinkably violent. The images of the scene haunt me, producing visions in my mind that leave me gasping for air as I imagine her terrified and alone, fighting to stay alive. I struggle to share the details with you because I know how difficult it was for me to hear. How her life ended is not what I want you to remember about my mother, but it is part of her story, and the truth of it must be shared.

These are the facts as I know them today: My mother went out for a fun night with girlfriends and never came home. At some point during the evening, they parted ways, each returning to her own home. None of the ladies who were with her that night have been forthcoming with the exact details surrounding the time or location of their goodbyes. To my knowledge, my mother did not stop at any local stores or gas stations after parting ways with her friends, and there is no record of her being seen alone at any point in the evening. With no detailed accounts as to how the evening ended, I am forced to assume that my mother said her goodbyes and was on her way home to us when things went terribly wrong.

Perhaps she was approached as she was walking to her car. Maybe another vehicle approached her, and she was lured off the road by someone, perhaps even someone she knew, or recognized from our small town. I don't know many young women who would willingly stop for a stranger in a situation like this, but I can't be sure that my mother wouldn't. My mother was kind. She loved people, and she may have acted out of the kindness of her heart, especially if she thought that a person needed help.

There is also a possibility that she met up with someone after leaving her girlfriends—someone that she knew—and things went sideways from there. I don't want to imagine this scenario, but I must consider it as a possibility. Maybe she met up with someone from the bank where she worked, or a regular customer that she had gotten to know.

I am an adult now, so I understand that people—even my mother—can find themselves in situations such as this. No one is perfect, and each of us is capable of making mistakes. The scenarios continue to build in my mind yet remain so unclear. There are no clear answers, and there likely never will be.

What I know for sure is that a monster raped my mother with the blunt end of an umbrella, then stabbed her in the chest with a small, sharp object just shy of a dozen times.

I don't know the sequence of events, but logic leads me to guess that she was raped first, while she was still alive, breathing, and fully aware of what was happening to her. The umbrella is an especially vile vision and one that will stick in your mind long after you finish reading this book. The inhumanity is unfathomable, and the pain she must have felt is unthinkable. The umbrella was a deliberate choice that her murderer made to cover their tracks. Whoever did this to her knew that raping her in the ordinary sense would leave behind physical evidence. I don't know what's worse; the fact that my mother was raped, or that it was done in such a horrifically violent manner. I only know that the scenes that my mind has created are seared there in cruel detail for all eternity.

My mother was found slouched down in the passenger side of her Toyota Sprint in the early morning hours of Sunday, August 23rd, 1987. Her car was on the far edge of a local carwash parking lot, not far from the main road. At the time it was unclear as to whether this was the place of her murder, or if she had been killed elsewhere and her car and body dumped here. Based on the crime scene photos and a basic understanding of forensics, I can assume that a crime of this nature would have required a remote location, out of sight and earshot. The killer would not wish to risk someone hearing my mother call for help, the primal, guttural sounds of her fighting for her life.

According to what I have been told, the car was not found as you would expect it if she had been killed inside. Perhaps there are details that I do not know, details that are too much for anyone to handle, so they have been kept quiet or omitted entirely— at least for my benefit. I know that there are some details yet to be revealed, likely at the trial.

If she had been stabbed while inside her vehicle, the sheer force of the instrument used and the location of the stab wounds would have resulted in excessive amounts of blood loss, creating a scene of such horror that my insides retch at the thought of it. According to reports, this was not the case. No, they would have taken her somewhere dark and remote, far away from the possibility of witnesses. I don't want to think of it: My mother, lying on the dewy grass, her body mangled, and spilling blood being picked up and placed into the passenger side of her car, slouched over and lifeless.

My mind recoils at the thought of her murderer then driving her to the place where she would be discovered, leaving her there all alone in the dark, cruel night.

It has always seemed odd to me that her killer took no measures to hide her body or the car. It was as if they wanted her to be found and wanted everyone to see what had been done to her. When she was found, it was determined that my mother had likely been dead for hours. Her lifeless body was drained; bleeding from the stab wounds having ceased hours before she was discovered.

The umbrella handle was unmistakably visible between her legs.

My father woke just as the sun was coming up, alarmed at the realization that my mother had not made it home the night before. He was not panicked; I mean, no one expects to find out that their wife and the mother of their only son is dead on the side of the road. He began calling a few people, asking if she had stayed with them for the night; however, no one had seen her or knew of her whereabouts. As panic began to set in, our doorbell rang. Two uniformed police officers calmly asked my father to sit down as they told him the life-changing news.

I was still peacefully asleep as this scene unfolded in the next room. This was my last night of peaceful sleep; my last night to dream sweet dreams of my family, forever forced to relive this last typical, normal, ordinary day. When my eyes slowly opened to the morning light, it was to a new chapter in my barely written story; the part where dreams end, and the nightmare begins.

Upon waking, I would have likely known that something was wrong. My mother was not there, and the police were in my house quietly talking to my father. Even a six-year-old would sense that something terrible must have happened. It would be unusual for my mother to be absent, so something terrible must have happened to her. My father would have told me to go to my room, but I most likely stood silently in the hallway listening to my father talk to the police.

I don't recall hearing the details of my mother's murder. I doubt that the police elaborated on the extent of the brutality during that initial visit. If they did, I either didn't hear it or blocked those memories, locking them away somewhere in the darkest chambers of my mind. If the latter is true, I am unable to retrieve the details of what I heard even today, as a grown man. In my research about childhood trauma, I have learned enough to know that these types of memories often get locked away in our minds, especially when the memory is too complex for a young mind to process. This is a common coping mechanism for trauma and is our brain's way of protecting us and allowing us to survive. At the age of six, there is no way that I would have been able to process the full weight of my mother's brutal murder. Truth be told, I am still processing it today—33 years later.

My very first vivid childhood memory is that of my father draping my small body over his lap as we cried out in sadness, each searching for words that did not exist. We stayed in this position for what seemed like an eternity; frozen, paralyzed with shock and profound loss. Mother. Wife. Our first love. Moving too soon would have made it real, and we weren't yet ready to face a world without her in it. We sobbed, weeping together until our eyes were swollen and dry. I cried every tear that I had within me that morning.

This is an intense first memory. Most kids' first memories involve holidays, birthdays, or special gifts. Not mine. Mine is about loss, crying out in profound sadness because I would never again see, hear, or feel my mother. The image of this memory is seared into my mind.

I have no idea what we did next. What does one even do after receiving life-shaking earth-shattering news such as this? If I had been older, I think we would have taken more time to grieve that morning. Maybe we would have decided to go into our own rooms and continue weeping quietly over our individual loss, lying in our beds all day, unable to move and drowning in grief and sorrow. Perhaps my father would have felt more comfortable sharing his feelings and inability to go through the motions if

I had been at an age to understand; but he knew that he must get up and continue living as normally as possible, for my sake. Things would never again be the same for either of us.

That morning our *new* normal began.

It's so fucked up that one day your life is completely normal, and the next your whole world can be torn apart. Things and people we love can be ripped away in an instant and yet the world just keeps on turning, the sun rising and setting just the same as it always has. It feels unfair, even cruel. I am keenly aware of this fact as an adult for having lived through this as a child.

We most likely ate something when the officers left, especially since it would have been late morning by this time. I picture myself sitting at our small kitchen table while my father silently went through the motions of making breakfast. How quickly life can change. Just yesterday we were all together in this very kitchen, happily eating breakfast, chatting, and laughing while preparing for a typical Saturday together as a family. Now, we are a family of two.

The fragility of life is almost unbearable. How can someone be there one day and gone forever the next? When your mother is suddenly gone and you *know* that she is never coming back the absence becomes instantly palpable, even for a six-year-old. I may not have had the language skills or vocabulary to adequately express the deep and changing nuances of my grief at the time, but simply put, I felt a deep emptiness.

Her absence instantly created a huge, gaping wound in our lives. The deep and engulfing sadness of our loss was—and still is—too overwhelming for words. What do you say when something like this happens to someone you love? To your wife? To your mother? My world was shattered into a million tiny pieces that could never be put back together. There were no clean cuts or lines that you could mend, even with the help of the strongest glue. It was completely shattered, imploded, with no recognizable pieces.

Words are incapable of capturing the depth of sorrow and despair that we felt. That *I* felt. There would be no more morning wake-up hugs and kisses, the perfect kind that only a mother can give. There would be no words of love and encouragement, voiced with gentle tones that only a mother knows how to offer. There would be no loving glances or gestures of adoration, expressions of a mother's perfect unconditional love.

These are all things that are critical to a son. One day she was there and life as I knew it was perfect. The next day she was gone. She was just gone. I still can't believe it, even as I write these words today. She. Is. Gone.

Nothing can take the place of a mother's love; nothing even comes close. Everything fails and fades in comparison. She will forever remain irreplaceable.

She is gone.

SELONIA

M y mother was born on December 13th, 1960, in Independence, Louisiana. It was a wintery day as a rare snowstorm swept through nearby Texas towns. The crisp 32-degree temperature was practically frigid compared to the typically tepid Louisiana winters and left icy dew on the grass and windowpanes.

It would have been difficult for her young parents to make it to the hospital in time. Motorists in Texas and Louisiana are not accustomed to icy roads, and the short drive would have been long and slow, with my grandmother praying all the way that they would make it in time. They made it—but *just*. My mother's birth was fast, with most of the labor occurring in the car while my grandfather drove.

They named her Selonia. Her name means *highland; an area of high or mountainous land; elevated above*. I'm not sure whether my grandparents chose her name because of its meaning, or simply because they liked the sound of it. Either way, it was perfect for her, poetic and lyrical. Selonia, elevated above, heavenly, and oth-er-worldly. It sounds like the tenderest yet most powerful ending note to a beautiful melody, and it is the most perfect name for my mother. I feel that it is even more so now, as I imagine her elevated high above, looking down on us, guiding us, protecting us, beaming with love and pride at all she helped to create.

From all accounts, she was an easy baby. Content. She loved to be held and rocked. She smiled and laughed earlier than most babies. She was a happy child and brought much joy to those around her. I often think about my mother as a baby when I am cradling and rocking my own son. He has her big, brown eyes. I wonder what my grandfather thought as he rocked her and looked into her eyes. I am certain that he beamed with love and had so many hopes and dreams for his daughter—my mother.

I know this because it is my experience with my son. The love is so deep that I can feel it in my bones. When I look into his eyes I see my mother, my father, and myself. We are all together once again in the depths of my son's beautiful brown eyes. They are so captivating, and I find myself staring deep and long into them, never wanting to look away. I want to soak up every ounce of this feeling of being together again with my mother and father.

Although her parents did not have a lot to offer her in the material sense, my mother was well-loved and cared for. She was raised to be loving, kind, and compassionate, and she was all those things. They excelled at raising an amazing daughter, sister, and eventually wife and mother. I cannot think of a better feeling as a parent than to see your daughter become the woman you always imagined she would be.

I had a mother that loved me with all her heart. I was the apple of her eye, and her pride and joy. She cared for me and adored me, more than anything else in the world. Many people never know this depth of love. Even though I don't have solid and tangible memories of her love, I know that it lives in my heart and is branded into my spirit. A mother's love is irreplaceable. It is like no other kind of love. This is especially true of the bond between a mother and her firstborn son. I see this love between my wife and our first son. It is a bond that can never be broken; it is completely unconditional. It is a pure love untouched by anything in the world. A mother would do anything for their son—anything.

My mother was a hard-working woman. Her work ethic and dedication to whatever she put her mind to allowed her the opportunity to work in the professions that she loved. She enjoyed serving others and interacting with colleagues and customers. She took pride in her work and did it well. She was beautiful and captivating. She possessed the kind of beauty that doesn't require anything extra—a natural beauty. Her skin was the perfect shade of brown. Her face was soft, and her eyes were deep, warm, and welcoming, turning upward on the outer edges when she smiled. When she smiled, she smiled with her whole face, and her smile could light up the darkest room. She was kind and gentle.

She was magic.

She made others feel seen, heard, and understood. She was a soft place to land. In a world filled with self-doubt, she made everyone feel better about themselves. She loved with her whole heart and mind—her whole *being*. She exuded love, so filled with it that it had no other option than to spill out and onto those around her. She had a way of making you feel like you were the only other person on the entire planet.

When you were with my mother, you felt like the shiniest star in the sky. She had a way of putting you at ease while at the same time making you feel like you could do anything you set your mind to, equal parts acceptance and encouragement. You could be exactly yourself with my mother, and she would accept you just as you were.

My mother held no judgments or agendas. She never set out to change another person. She accepted, loved, and acknowledged people, which is a rare quality. There was no one else like her; a truly unique and special gift to everyone she touched. She always offered an easy smile and laugh. Her smile and laughter were infectious. People loved being in my mother's presence. She was a good friend, always putting others before herself. She truly wanted to know others. She went deep with people, never skimming the surface of relationships. If you were in my mother's life, she *knew* you—your deepest thoughts and emotions— and you felt safe with her.

I realize that all this paints her as absolute perfection. As an adult, I know that cannot be true. I must recognize the fact that she—like all of us—had flaws and imperfections.

But *I* will not remember her that way.

She is my mother and will live forever perfect in my mind, and my heart.

THE INTERROGATION

I may not have concrete memories from this day, but I do have a video. There is raw, slightly pixilated footage of me, a small child, being interrogated. It is hard to describe the feeling of watching yourself experience something like this without having any actual memory of it. It's surreal on so many levels.

Watching your six-year-old self being interrogated by the police is not like watching a video of yourself riding a bike for the first time or playing in your first baseball tournament. The emotions that it brings are real and raw. I feel both sorry and anxious for the boy I see—for *me*. No child should be forced to go through such an experience, especially so soon after their mother has been taken. It is hard for me to watch; seeing the nervous energy and hearing my small voice answering the questions the best I knew how.

The video opens with my grandfather and godmother sitting side by side in chairs that are pushed against the back wall. It is a tiny room; sterile, and cold, with only a clock on the back wall. My grandfather appears as if he has been there a while. He is slumped in his chair, legs stretched out in front of him and crossed at the ankles. My godmother sits upright, legs crossed. They both are dressed nicely, presumably in their Sunday church clothes. My father and I are seated on the opposite side of the room, but do not appear on camera.

The investigator is a middle-aged Black woman. She sits on the floor, her back against the wall with both legs stretched out in front of her. She is not wearing shoes. This is so odd. Why is she barefoot? Was this some attempt to make us feel more comfortable, as if we were at home? The investigator begins by trying to separate me from my father, and it becomes clear why we are all here. Speaking in a sing-song tone, she uses every tool in her repertoire to make me open up and become comfortable enough to speak to her alone—without my father. It is clear I'm not interested in her or anything she has to say. It is also clear that I am not going anywhere without my father.

She asks if I like football, and I hear my voice, small and innocent, for the first time.

"Yeah."

"Do you like the Saints," she asks.

I don't answer. I doubt if I had any idea who the Saints were, nor did I care. My idea of football was tossing the ball around with my friends. She tells me she can take me to meet all the Saint's players.

"Would you like that? To meet some NFL players? They're big guys like your daddy. Would you like to go with me? I know they'd love to meet you."

Again, I don't answer. She stands up looking frustrated and goes off-camera.

My grandfather mutters under his breath. "That boy isn't going anywhere without his dad. She's wasting her time."

He was right. My grandfather becomes visibly irritated, rubbing his face and squirming in his seat. The investigator returns and asks me directly to speak with her alone, without my father.

"It'll be okay. I'm your friend, I promise," she says.

My father echoes her. "It's okay. I'll be right outside if you need me."

No go. She is going to have to speak to me with my father present. My grandfather and godmother stand to leave, and my father and I take their seats on the back wall.

I see myself for the first time.

I am casually but neatly dressed in jeans, a tucked-in t-shirt, and bright white tennis shoes. My father is well-dressed, as was his way. He is wearing dark colored dress pants, a long-sleeved pinstriped button-down shirt with an oversized collar, shiny wing-tipped shoes, and a fedora. I fiddle nervously with a white paper cup. I assume they gave me water before we began. The cup is now empty, and I lift it into the air, spiraling it down and back up again in an effort to distract myself from the discomfort of the moment.

The investigator begins with surface-level questions, once again trying to make me relax and feel more comfortable. She asks me about school and whether I like it or not. I answer her questions in short responses. I do not elaborate on details or get carried away with a story like many kids would if asked a generalized question. It is clear from the very beginning that I don't want to be there, and I absolutely do not want to answer her questions. She asks me about my friends.

"Do you have a lot of friends?"

I nod.

"Who's your best friend?"

"My daddy," I answer quickly. My tone is so innocent.

It is clear this is not the answer she wants or expects, and she quickly moves on to another topic. Our close relationship is evident to her already. My father and I are sitting next to each other, but I shift, moving my body so close to my father that I am partially sitting on his chair. I look at him when she questions me, and he touches my cheek or leg, soothing and encouraging me.

"It's alright . . . just answer the questions. You're okay."

This goes on for about thirty minutes as she asks more surface questions. She continues to try to get me to open up and talk more about school, friends, desserts—anything. She does everything she can to get me to relax and respond to her, but nothing works. I remain glued to my father's side and keep my answers brief. About mid-way through the interrogation, she tries once again to interview me alone, seeking to separate me from my father. I assume she was not getting what she wanted or needed so she wanted to try questioning me without my father by my side. She and I stand up and walk out of the room, but quickly return. I refused to leave my father's side. If she was going to continue interviewing me, it was going to have to be alongside my father.

She lights up a cigarette, perhaps feeling stressed or frustrated at her inability to get me to interact with her. Anyone can see by my body language that I don't like the fact that she is smoking. I put more distance between her and myself. She asks if I don't like the smoke, and I confidently reply "no." I didn't like any of it, but I especially hated the smell of her cigarette in the tiny, enclosed room.

She apologizes and stamps the cigarette out, continuing with her questioning. She begins to ask more specific questions about the day that my mom was murdered. She asks what we did that day, and I tell her we went to the mall. We talk about the cookie, and she elaborates about her love for the cookies at the mall and sharing them with her daughter. It is so obvious that she wants me to carry on elaborating as she models the type of conversation that she is trying to create with me.

I am still not having any part of it. My answers remain brief, and I move my small body closer and closer to my father. About forty-five minutes into the interview, she asks about my mother. I become visibly uncomfortable. I shift in my chair, standing up and sitting back down. I don't want to be questioned about my mom. She ignores my obvious cues to back off. Maybe she doesn't care that I am clearly rattled, upset, and uncomfortable, because she has a job to do, and that job is to get me to talk. Her job is to get me to reveal something that would identify the person who killed my mother, or perhaps even incriminate my father.

She continues to pry, and I begin shutting down. Who wouldn't? I am a six-year-old boy who just lost his mother. I don't want to be in this small, sterile space being questioned by anyone, especially not her.

The situation unravels and I begin to cry. I tell her that I don't want to talk anymore, and my father repeats my sentiments. She continues. Perhaps this is where she wants me, upset, crying, vulnerable, the perfect opportunity to get me to voice the things she hopes I will say. My father straightens in his seat, becoming visibly protective of me. His next words are stern.

"That's enough. No More. He's done." He comforts and soothes me with a kiss on the forehead. "It's okay," he says. "It's okay."

It is *not* okay.

Nothing is okay.

Watching this now, I feel a surge of emotions. As a grown man, I can clearly see what she was trying to do to me and it isn't right, or okay. It makes me sad and angry at the same time. I feel like I want to reach into the screen and scoop this little boy up and rescue him from this awful situation.

This little boy is me. He is still very much a part of me.

Six-year-old boys who have just lost their mother should not have to endure a police interrogation, regardless of how relaxed she tried to make it seem. They were trying to get something out of me—information that I did not have. Whether they thought I knew something and I would relax enough to reveal it, that I would crack under the pressure and give them what they wanted, they didn't get what they were seeking from me this day.

We complied fully with the police in the months after as they investigated my mother's murder. We showed up to every interview. I believe there was at least one more interview between me and an investigator; however, this is the only video I have. I have no memory of this or any other interviews besides what I see in the video. I know they likely questioned my father in this way many times in the months after her death.

According to the police, they conducted a full investigation. Investigators documented that they "turned over every rock and interviewed every possible person who may have information." There were no more leads, and their investigation ran dry. Months later they were no closer to revealing the identity of my mother's killer than they were at the very beginning. I don't know the exact end date of their investigation but at some point, they closed my mother's case. They had come to the end of their search for her killer and had decided that nothing else could be done.

Case closed.

My mother's murder was officially a *cold case*.

COLD CASE

The dictionary defines a cold case as an unsolved criminal investigation which remains open pending the discovery of new evidence, *unsolved* being the operative word.

After months of active investigation, my mother's murder had become a cold case. Her death was a mystery, without resolution or closure for her grieving family. However, I think you know as well as I do that nothing is ever a complete and total mystery. Someone out there always knows something. It is possible that many people know many things about my mother's whereabouts on that fateful night, perhaps even the details of her final moments. I don't believe a case is ever truly cold. Someone killed her, and that means that *someone* knows the truth and holds the key to unlocking the whole case; someone out there knows every single detail.

The person or persons who killed her—or looked on while she was being killed—know exactly what the police were unable to uncover. I suppose I have always held out hope that eventually the case will be solved, and that the authorities will discover new information that will lead them to her killer. I have never been able to reconcile the fact that someone got away with such a heinous crime.

Also, people are generally terrible at keeping secrets. As the saying goes, *people talk*, and in the case of criminal activity this is mostly because they cannot carry the burden of committing such terrible acts. So, even though the police labeled my mother's case *cold* more than three decades ago, I have always held out hope that her killer would eventually be found, and that someone would break under the pressure of their guilt. I have hoped that someone is out there drowning in guilt and shame, every day moving closer to the point of confessing.

That day has never come.

I have endured decades of silence.

There has been no further investigation into my mother's murder; nothing new and no fresh information.

Until June of 2019.

On Friday, June 22nd, I received the panicked phone call that would change my life once again. The police had arrested my father for my mother's murder, thirty-two years later. They went to my father's house—my childhood home—and took him into custody, stating that new information had been uncovered which linked him to the murder. I was shocked, confused, and hurt. Most of all, I was angry. I am *still* angry. My mind churned with questions. What could they possibly have on my father *now* that they did not have on him at the time of the murder?

The pain and horror of my mother's death came flooding in, once again. It was as if no time had passed, and I was again a six-year-old boy losing his parent. I cannot adequately express how heavy the time between my father's arrest and his trial has weighed on me, knowing every day that my father's fate is hanging in the balance.

Someone recently asked me, which was harder, losing my mom as a child or losing my father as an adult. The truth is, it has been more difficult to lose my father—my rock. This feels wrong to feel, and even more so to admit. I feel guilty over my answer, and I know some will not understand. that the fact of the matter is that I have had 39 years of life with my father. As sad and tragic as my mother's death was and still is, I had only six short years with her. Beyond this, my memories of my mother are intangible, even hazy, and often coming in bits and pieces. There are times when I don't know whether my memories are real, or a fabrication of the recollections of others. I was simply too young.

Try to think back; what is your earliest childhood memory? How old were you? Can you recall specific experiences and inter-actions with your parents when you were six years old? Do you recall times spent with your mother, or have specific memories from this young age? It is most likely that you do not. You may have retained bits and pieces just as I have, but we really don't start forming solid long-term memories until later in our developmental process.

So, my answer to the question of which loss has been harder on me is this: The loss of my dad. That is not to say that the loss of my mother is not interwoven within the loss that I feel today. I feel the loss of my father more deeply *because* of the events of my young childhood. My father and I are solidly bonded because of the loss of my mother. Perhaps the answer is not that the loss of my father is *more* difficult; maybe it is not an either/or scenario. Maybe the truest answer is both, because in truth they cannot really be separated.

My mother is a part of my father. He was forced to step into her role after her death. He became both mother and father to me. This means that losing my dad today is like losing him and losing my mother all over again. It is deep and complex, and it is hard for me to explain in words. All I know is that when the police came and took him away on that day in June, I felt very much like the six-year-old boy who had just lost his mother. I was lost. Untethered. I had no control over what was happening, and there was nothing that I could do. I felt completely helpless.

As I write this, my father is awaiting trial as an inmate in Tangipahoa Parish prison. We have no idea how long he will be there, and as of today no date has been set for his trial. He has been assigned a public defender who seems to care very much about him and his case. I speak to him as often as I can. My father never complains, grumbles, or expresses any kind of discomfort. He is in prison and yet he is still filled with positivity. He always makes sure it is a good time for us to talk, always thinking about me above himself. He asks about me, my wife, my son—his only grandson—and never talks about what he is going through. He is simply making the best of a terrible situation.

My father is a man of great faith. He attributes his inner peace and joy to his relationship with God. He trusts God and his plan. My father has become a sort of mentor to the younger inmates, finding great meaning in speaking into their lives. They see him reading his Bible and they ask questions. They see a peace in him and want it for themselves. He holds daily scripture readings among the inmates and tells me that some of these men have never read the Bible. My father reads and explains the scriptures to them and tells them of the hope that it brings. He encourages them to read the Bible aloud in their group. He is ministering to others while in the worst possible situation. It is truly remarkable.

My father reminds me of the story of Paul from the Bible. Paul was imprisoned, shackled and in chains in a dark cave. However, far from being hardened or bitter over his circumstances, we see a wonderfully warm and tender man, always expressing love and concern for others over himself. Paul writes that though he is a prisoner, his soul is freer than ever before. If there is one thing that is clear from the story of Paul, it is that he has a deep abiding joy despite his circumstances. When his situation looked less than promising, Paul was jubilant and joyful. His love and care for others kept him alive and filled with hope, even in his darkest moments.

My father is much like Paul in that although his present circumstances are bleak and the outcome unknown, he remains filled with a desire to help others through his own deep core of hope and joy. This is the hope that can always be found in my story. My father is not angry, bitter, or resentful. I cannot say that I would be as content under the same circumstances. I would wager to say that most people would not.

My father's hope and joy are untouchable and are not dictated by his circumstances. He never asks why or gives way to self-pity. He never questions God. He says that he cannot because questioning Him would be like a betrayal. He is clear that God has been so good to him, bringing him through the worst days of his life. He knows God will uphold him, and sustain him under any circumstance, always providing exactly what he needs.

There is a deep peace in his voice when we speak. It is so hard for me to imagine him in prison, but it brings me some comfort to know that he is content. There is hope in his voice. He looks for the positive—the silver lining—in every situation. As difficult it is for me to imagine him there as a prisoner, I follow his lead and I too search for the good. My father tells me that God has and always will be faithful, so I borrow and share his faith with confidence that good things will come.

This keeps me afloat. This keeps me from sinking.

And for now, this is enough.

NEW NORMAL

In the days, weeks, and months following my mother's murder, my father and I were forced to pick ourselves up and out of our grief and find our new way of living without my mother. It is so strange to have someone living beside you every day, and then one day they are no longer there. It is much like losing a limb. It feels as if they should be there, and sometimes you even expect to hear their voice or see them round a corner. The loss and absence are heavy.

I don't understand how the world keeps spinning, or the sun keeps rising and setting after such terrible loss. The world should stop for a bit, with the sun frozen in place. This never happens, even under the worst of circumstances. The world keeps spinning, and the sun keeps rising and setting. The world goes on.

It feels like a bit of a betrayal. The seasons change and the days turn into weeks, and finally into months and years. I wish I could have stopped time to truly process the loss my father and I were feeling. I wish I could have pressed pause. We needed time.

It is a cruel truth, but you must just keep moving on. The universe does not recognize our need to stop and make sense of what has happened. People die all the time. Every second. As I write this someone is dying. People are saying their last good-byes to loved ones. Someone is receiving the worst news of their life, news that their loved one has been taken.

There is nothing unique about my situation. Mothers die. However, somehow when it is *you* that bears the weight of such a loss, it seems unfair, as if no one else in the entire whole world understands the kind of pain you are feeling. Despite the pain, my father and I kept moving, bearing the weight but moving as best we knew how.

My father endured questioning from the police in the weeks that followed my mother's death. I cannot imagine how he dealt with the scrutiny of the police on top of the sorrow and grief he was carrying. But he did, all while taking care of me. I am sure that he was initially a person of interest—the spouse always is. I am certain that the police and investigators dissected every part of my parent's relationship. Police questioning is intense, and a normal marriage with all its ups and downs looks quite different under the microscope of police interrogation.

"Did you fight?"

"Did you ever yell at one another?"

"Were you happily married?"

"Were you romantically involved with anyone other than your wife?"

"Was she seeing anyone outside of the marriage?"

This must have been brutal. Your wife is dead, they think you may have killed her, and you are forced to try and convince them otherwise. It must have been an impossible situation, but my father endured. He showed up on time, nicely dressed and prepared for every interview. He cooperated fully with the investigation. He answered every question and provided all that was asked of him. He told them the truth: Their marriage was not perfect, but then, no marriage is. Even so, they loved one another deeply. He would never hurt my mother, and he would never do anything that would hurt me.

Days turned into weeks and weeks into months. Summer gave way to fall, and the police still had nothing. They were no closer to finding my mother's killer than they were when they first began. There was no solid physical evidence despite the brutality of the crime, nor were there any eyewitness testimonies leading the police in the right direction. It was the 1980s, which meant that the forensic capabilities of the investigative team were not what they are today.

Eventually, my mother's case was closed. The police had nowhere else to look. They had turned over every stone and asked every question, and still had nothing. There would be no closure for me and my father. This fact compounded our grief, and the mystery of her death hung heavy in our small community. It was utterly inexplicable. How does something like this happen? How does someone get away with murdering a young wife and mother? How is it that no one saw *anything*?

My father and I would live our lives in this unresolved tension, without answers or closure. We would get up every morning and go to bed every night, never knowing who took her from us. I cannot explain to you what this lack of closure—on top of grieving the death of your mother—does to a young boy. I am only now beginning to peel back the layers of that time in my life.

From what I have learned about childhood loss and trauma, my six-year-old self began compartmentalizing the pain and suffering, creating a new normal in which I could move on with my life.

In order to survive, I had to shove things deep into the recesses of my mind and heart. I could not live everyday as a young boy with my mother's death in the forefront of my mind. This would have completely overtaken and consumed me. Compartmentalizing was not a conscious act; six-year-old boys do not typically know how to do such a thing. Compartmentalizing happens unconsciously. It is the body and mind's way of protecting itself in order to survive.

At six years old, survival mode became my *only* mode.

I knew nothing different.

I had not been given the opportunity to live any other way.

This unthinkable tragedy and the corresponding trauma have informed everything in my life. I grew up existing in survival mode, and I still live very much the same way today. I don't know any other way, although I am trying. This book is part of that effort; telling my story and sharing my truth is part of breaking free from the confines of survival and moving into a life of abundance in which I can finally experience the joy of thriving. This is no small feat. Patterns and behaviors are difficult to unlearn. I have lived in this space for so long that it is hard for me to even recognize all the areas and ways in which my life has been impacted.

This is not to say that I have not lived. I have lived. I have lived a great life despite all that I have been through; but there is a part of myself still yearning to be free. I know that even though I have a wonderful, successful life there is still so much waiting for me to uncover. The six-year-old boy inside of me needs to be expressed for the adult me to be free.

I am doing the work, and I am asking hard questions. I am reflecting on my life, talking, and thinking about my mother's death more than I ever have before. Reflecting and talking is helpful, and I am beginning to see the threads that have run through every circumstance and experience in my life. Though I have not spent every day feeling the burden of losing my mother, the effects of that loss have created a certain pattern of living.

I have learned, by way of necessity, the art of coping. Coping mechanisms are how I live—how I survive. They show up in various forms; however, the end goal is always the same: *How do I survive?* I have placed limits throughout my life, which is a common effect of childhood loss and trauma. I unintentionally limit myself in almost every area of my life. This is a coping mechanism, part of survival mode, and a way of protecting myself from more pain and loss.

This is no way to live. I know that I deserve more from life. The people that I love deserve more from me. I am tired of living this way. I am ready, willing, and eager to do whatever it takes to live an abundant life. I can't undo the past, but I can take control of my future. I can decide not to allow my past to dictate the way that I live any longer. When I was a boy and a young man, I didn't know there was any other way. I thought that to simply survive was just fine.

Maya Angelou once said, "When you know better, you do better." I know better now. I have enough distance from the trauma to see that the way that I have been living is no longer sustainable for me and my family. I don't want to repeat the lessons of my past with my own son. I must break this cycle. I *will* break this cycle.

The cycle ends with me.

MY FATHER

My father has always been—and will always be—my hero. As a little boy, I looked up to him. *Once a Marine, always a Marine*, he remained strong, capable, successful, and a wonderful role model. He loved and respected others and was loved and respected in return. My father was a strong figure in our community, and people valued his opinions and contributions. As a young boy, I *felt* this. I very much wanted to be strong, capable, and well respected, like my father.

This did not change after my mother's death. I still looked up to him—possibly even more so. I cannot imagine what he must have been going through in the early weeks and months after losing my mother. I imagine he was completely heartbroken at the loss of his first love; his wife and partner in caring for and parenting me. I imagine that he was barely making it through each day, the weight of sadness and loss bearing down on him.

But he never let me see it.

He was strong for me. He *chose* to be strong for me.

My father could have easily crumbled under his own pain and grief. He could have lain in the bed day after day, longing for my mother, unable to do the everyday things in life let alone raise a son. He could have easily made the decision to leave me to be raised by my grandmother. No one would have blamed him. In the 1980s being a single father was not commonplace, especially under our circumstances. But he never wavered in his decision to stay. Looking back now, as a grown man with my own young son, this fills me with deep respect, compassion, and gratitude.

My father stayed—for me. That is the very definition of love and dedication.

In the absence of my mother my father became my North Star, the guiding light and force in my young life and my safe place of refuge from the world. My father became my whole life—my everything. From the very beginning, my father began parenting me in specific ways in which to ensure that I would be able to stand confidently on my own two feet as a grown man. His parenting was solid, consistent, and at times, overly strict. The boundaries were clear; I knew exactly what to expect and what was expected of me. There was no guessing about what was allowed, and what wasn't.

My father was a very detail oriented and structured parent. His expectations were high, and often hard to reach. He consistently set the bar higher and higher. He provided structure when it would have been very easy for him to just wing it or go easy on me *because* I had lost my mother. It was quite the opposite, in fact. I think he took the job of parenting me even more seriously because I had lost my mother. He was not an absent parent. He was involved and engaged in every aspect of my life.

He made sure that I continued to attend private school, which was a huge financial sacrifice. He understood the value of a good education and made sure I was surrounded by the best teachers. On top of my education at Holy Ghost Catholic School, my father created an atmosphere of learning within our home. My father was tough in this way, and he expected a lot from me, even as a young boy.

At the time I did not understand. His expectations often seemed harsh, and oftentimes unattainable. Sometimes it even felt like a punishment, especially to a young boy who was more interested in going outside with friends or playing video games. Everything felt like a test, and one which I never felt like I was passing. Most of the time, I assumed I was failing—failing him, and failing myself. I struggled with simply feeling good enough for my father. It was not easy to think that I was letting him down, or not living up to his expectations.

Reading was one of the things we consistently worked on. He would choose something for me—typically a book or text way above my reading and comprehension level— and he would have me read aloud to him. Some days it was Newsweek magazine, other days the daily newspaper. Sometimes I read the dictionary. The point is, I never got to read anything that I was actually interested in. I felt nervous when I read to him. I often began in a shy tone, but he would quickly tell me to "speak up." If I stumbled over a word, he would have me repeat the word, and oftentimes look it up in the dictionary.

He would monitor my eye contact as well. If I did not look up periodically and make eye contact, he would remind me, "Look up, Reggie! Make eye contact!" I never felt like I was doing it correctly. Sometimes my voice would shake, and my palms would sweat. I never felt like I was living up to his expectation.

My father allowed me to experience and feel the tension— the nerves. He had a clear goal in his mind, and so he carried on despite how uncomfortable it made me feel. It was difficult, but I did it. This became part of our new normal routine. He was adamant that I would be confident in speaking in front of other people. It is amazing to me that I did grow in confidence, especially under strict scrutiny of my every word. I suppose as uncomfortable as it was, some of this training stuck and much of it worked. I could not see it then. Then, it just felt awful—like the worst kind of punishment.

I see everything more clearly now. Hindsight—in addition to fatherhood—has given me a perspective that I did not have as a child. My father had his reasons. He wasn't hard on me just for the sake of being hard. He was hard on me because he wanted me to be strong, capable, and to have the tools and experiences that I would need as a man. It was his way of ensuring that despite everything, I would be okay. I would be able to survive in the world. Now, I understand exactly what he was doing. I understand his motivations and his commitment to fathering me into a confident young man and successful adult. In many ways, I attribute my past and present success to my father. For this, I am so grateful.

His insistence that I feel confident speaking in front of other people is the basis of my career. Today, I can speak confidently to large groups of people—professionals and doctors at the top of their field. I speak clearly, without the nervousness that most people deal with regarding public speaking. I use the proper into-nations, I do not stumble over my words, and I know when to look up and make eye contact with the audience. I do not know if I could do this without those countless hours of reading time as a young boy. It felt like hell at times, but I am thankful that he taught me the value of confident communication.

I wish I could tell you that these sessions instilled a love of reading in me. While I am a great communicator, confident in front of crowds, and have even loved the process of writing this book—I still hate reading. Maybe I always would have hated it even without the pressure my dad placed on reading. Who knows? The fact remains that I hate to read.

My father kept close tabs on me growing up and reading was just a small part of this. He let me have some freedom, but the boundaries were always in place and clearly communicated. I didn't dare step out of line with my father. I knew not to test him. Above everything else, I wanted to please him. I wanted him to be proud of me. As I reflect on my childhood, the dominant emotions that I feel are gratitude and hope. My father was doing the best he knew how, and ultimately, he did a great job. I do not know many single fathers who are as committed as he was to me. I know that he did everything in my best interest, and that I was his driving force.

There is an immense amount of hope to be taken from how my father rose up and did what he needed to do to be the best father he could be for me. Hope that even in the darkest situations, the human spirit compels us to rise, fight, and to keep putting one foot in front of the other. My father's story—our story—is one of rising up, of hoping against hope that if you get up each day and do the best that you can, everything will ultimately be okay.

Despite everything, and even on our darkest days, we were okay.

I said before that my father was my North Star and my guiding force. I realize now that I was *his* North Star, too. We were bonded by our pain. The loss of my mother sealed our bond. We trusted and relied on one another for nearly everything. We grew up together and learned how to live as best we could without her. My father needed me as much as I needed him.

We were the only two people in the world who could completely understand what the other was feeling. There is great comfort in that. I knew he understood. I never had to explain, because he just *knew*. I pray that I offered the same level of comfort to him. I think that I did. He knew I understood, and that he never had to explain, because I just knew. This type of bond is sealed, solid, and forged to stand the test of time.

Our bond is unmovable. Unshakable.

And it will never be broken.

STRUCTURE AND SCAFFOLDING

There was no lack of structure in my life as a boy. My father was a master at building structure, creating boundaries, and enforcing discipline in our lives—in *my* life. I believe this is how he was able to successfully parent me despite being a young, single father. Structure made life more predictable. He knew exactly how our days would unfold. He left nothing up to chance. He knew that he would be able to carry on as long as life unfolded exactly according to his plan.

This was not always easy for me. Sometimes I felt smothered, suffocated, walled in by so much *structure*. There was not much freedom to explore outside the boundaries that my father had built, or avenues to test what life was like without these walls.

He built walls to keep me safe, and in turn to keep himself safe from further loss and heartbreak. He taught me how to survive day to day; but eventually, as I grew a bit older, I began to feel stifled. I needed to explore the world on my own, without the safety nets he had installed around me.

I needed room to take chances.

I needed to take risks.

I needed to dream.

I needed my mother. My mother was the scaffolding that I so needed. She was the encourager, the dreamer. She was an eternal optimist, a quiet yet powerful voice telling me that I could do anything I set my mind to. Without the balance of having both father and mother—structure and scaffolding—I was left feeling imprisoned by the walls.

If my mother had been there, she would have slowly built the scaffolding before the walls. She would have encouraged me to climb the scaffolding, then to peek out over the walls and see all the possibilities life had to offer me. She wouldn't have let me get too far, always a step or two below me just in case I fell. If my mother had lived my parents would have been a power couple, the perfect blend of dynamic parenting. Together they would have built structure and order, with a healthy dose of encouragement and inspiration to dream.

My whole childhood would have been different if she had lived.

I imagine my mother lifting me up on her shoulders: *"Look Reggie! Look at the big, beautiful world out there . . . Do you see it? You are going to do amazing things. The world is waiting on you!"* I would believe her and trust her. I would feel alive with the possibilities, a small fire kindled in my heart for all the magic the world contained just for me, waiting for me to make my own unique mark.

She was the magic.

This is in stark contrast to how I imagine this same scene with my father: *"Look Reggie, look at the big world just waiting to chew you up and spit you out."* I would believe him and trust him. I would feel afraid, shrinking back in fear of a world too scary and unpredictable to experience. Kids need balance, a good measure of magic and reality.

I didn't have that balance.

Everything was fear, and protect yourself, and uncertainty. There was no magic. There was no room for the beautiful possibilities. I wonder how my life might be different had I grown up with fewer boundaries.

Keep kicking the can. Just keep kicking the can is one of the mantras I have developed over the years. The visual is me, a variation of ages in my mind, kicking an empty aluminum soda can. My head is down, eyes intensely focused. I square the toes of my shoe up to the can and kick; not too hard as I need to maintain control, keeping my eyes on it as it bounces and skids along the gravel. I walk forward, eyes never leaving the can, and kick again.

And again.

And again.

This is my life.

I have always felt as though I had to just keep kicking the can. Keep things moving. Don't linger on anything too long. Don't allow too much time to gather in my mind. This focus has allowed me to become successful in many areas of my life, but I wonder what I may have missed out on—what I am still missing out on—because my eyes are down and focused solely on the can.

Keep moving it forward.

Eyes down. Squared toes.

Kick.

Eyes down. Squared toes.

Kick.

CHILDHOOD TRAUMA

"Childhood trauma can lead to an adulthood spent in survival mode, afraid to plant roots, to plan for your future, to trust, to let joy in."
—DR. THELMA BRYANT-DAVIS

I t took me a very long time to admit that I endured a childhood trauma, even to myself. As I wrote the heading for this chapter my stomach flip-flopped a bit, making me unsure if I should share and wondering if this part of my story even matters. Doubt and questioning are part of the trauma. I don't know why it is so hard to admit or share this fact with others. For a long time, I thought that admitting that I had experienced childhood trauma meant that I was weak or broken on the inside. Or perhaps acknowledging the trauma and how it has affected me all these years would make everything too real for me.

I am still not completely comfortable with my trauma, and I don't know if I will ever be. I don't like it, and I especially do not like looking at it, or talking about it. I never linger too long on thoughts surrounding my trauma. This is uncomfortable for me. It is much easier for me to put it in the box where it has been hidden away inside of me and keep moving forward.

But I am in the process of healing, so here goes:

The trauma of my mother's murder is time-stamped on both my body and my brain. It has become part of my DNA. Although I have no outward gaping wounds or scars visible for the world to see and understand, I am, in fact, wounded. I am scarred. My wounds are hidden deep within me, often invisible even to myself. Trauma is especially difficult because so often there are no visible wounds to tend to. This would be easier if I had a broken arm or leg, and people could see the wound. They would offer help, understand my pain, and know the process of healing a broken limb. Inner wounds often go undetected, making them easy to compartmentalize and ignore.

My pain has not manifested into outward struggles like many who have been through childhood trauma, a fact which makes them especially easy to overlook. That is not to say that I don't have outward struggles—I certainly have my share. Luckily mine are not overt, like addiction, depression, anxiety, or health issues. My trauma is more subtle. It sits right below the surface, patched over, and covered by layers of bandages and decades of coping. Emotional trauma is unseen—tricky. It is like an invisible thief that constantly attempts to steal parts of my life; not in one fell swoop, but daily, bit by bit. All at once would be too obvious. I would be forced to face it head-on. It is more nuanced, ebbing and flowing, allowing me to look away rather than deal with it. My trauma steals just enough to keep me wounded, but not enough to motivate me to pursue true healing.

This is how I have been able to survive under the weight thus far. It surfaces in bits and pieces here and there, which makes it bearable and tricks me into soldiering on, pushing through, moving forward despite how I am feeling. It tells lies like, *that's just how you were raised,* and *this is just who you are.* These lies are easy to believe because there is an element of truth within each of them. It is easier to believe the lies than to truly examine our wounds. Our learned behaviors are formed from trauma, and we must dig deep to find the roots.

My trauma has become a part of me. It is always with me, which means that I can never escape it for too long. As I get older it demands to be uncovered and explored. My body and mind have had enough. I feel as if I simply cannot carry it any longer without experiencing some major health impacts.

In the book *The Body Keeps the Score*, author Bessel A. Van der Kolk writes: *"We have learned that trauma is not just an event that took place sometime in the past; it is also the imprint left by that experience on mind, brain, and body. This imprint has ongoing consequences for how the human organism manages to survive in the present. Trauma results in a fundamental reorganization of the way mind and brain manage perceptions. It changes not only how we think and what we think about, but also our very capacity to think."*

We can run and hide from our trauma for only so long. Eventually, it will catch us, totally cutting us off at the knees and leaving us incapable of living a life filled with the things we desire—what we deserve. The body is usually the first to show symptoms of overload. As the title of Van der Kolk's book says, *the body keeps the score*. Trauma is not benign. It will have its way eventually, especially if we ignore it for too long. This means that I must continue to do the work. There is too much at stake, as this is no longer just about me. I must heal in order to be all that I am meant to be for myself and for the people I love. I hope that by exploring and exposing my trauma—my wounds and scars—I can begin to truly heal. It is also my hope that by sharing my experience I will help others begin to confront and heal from their own inner trauma.

Trauma does not have to be the loss of a parent. It comes in all forms and in all shapes and sizes. It looks different to everyone, and the path to healing is unique for every person. There is no single sure-fire prescription for healing from trauma. It is not a game of connecting the dots, because the dots may never connect. What I do know is this: There is so much hope for healing. People who have endured trauma and are still living life and doing good work in the world are some of the strongest people we know. I recognize that experiencing trauma and in turn healing, oftentimes makes people stronger, more resilient, compassionate, and better able to empathize with others. There is something about experiencing the most extreme depths of suffering that motivates people to become all that they were made to be. Life becomes more precious, and nothing is taken for granted.

It is hard for me to extend this grace and recognition to myself, but I can see it in others. I know others see it in me, but I just cannot see it—yet. When I asked a few close friends how they view me as a person one of the words that I kept hearing was *resilient*. They see in me what I do not see but want to. They have shared that they have no idea how I was able to endure such a loss and still carry on. They say they see me as *strong*, and able to deal with anything that comes my way. They see me as an *overcomer* and someone who has been able to conquer their pain and become a better person because of it.

I hope as I journey along this path of healing, I will someday see myself as this strong, resilient, compassionate person, deeply connected to the world and to the people I love.

Perhaps this is just around the corner for me.

HOLY GHOST CATHOLIC SCHOOL

I could have easily attended the public school in our neighborhood. That's where all the neighborhood kids went. I could have ridden the bus to and from school just like the other kids, but my mother and father wanted me to get a better education than the public school could provide. They feared I would get lost in a sea of my peers and not receive the individual attention students deserve in school. They both valued a good education, and I suppose they were doing for me what their own parents were unable to do for them.

My parents sacrificed a great deal to enroll me in private school. I attended Holy Ghost Catholic School from kindergarten through the end of my sixth-grade year. There was no bus to pick me up, so my father drove me to school every morning. As a parent myself, I now see that this was also a great sacrifice.

I was not the most prolific student. I don't recall my early years at Holy Ghost, but I do remember the ones after my mother's death. School was never easy for me, and I struggled in many ways. I don't know if this was because I had lost my mother, but it's likely. Most children who experience trauma report having trouble in school. Many young people with childhood trauma—childhood post-traumatic stress disorder—report having behavior issues such as anger and rage that stem from unresolved emotions surrounding their trauma. Many experience failing grades, ADD, ADHD, bullying, and much more.

I had a great deal of trouble concentrating. I recall feeling disconnected from what was going on around me. The teachers called this *daydreaming*, and I did a lot of daydreaming. The lessons did not hold my attention for very long, and before I knew it my eyes would wander out the window and my mind floated a million miles away.

I was one of just a handful of Black students at Holy Ghost, and that handful included my older cousins. It was not typical for Black kids to attend private school. I don't specifically recall not fitting in with the other students, although I am sure this played a part in my scholastic difficulties. There was no one who looked like me in my class, or my grade. I think this affects kids, especially since they spend such a large part of their life at school.

I was never overtly bullied. I do recall being called "the nigger" once by a fellow male student, but it was not an everyday thing. The students likely accepted me because of my father's reputation within the community. He rubbed shoulders at community events with many of my peer's parents and was well-respected by the church. My grandfather—my father's dad—opened the doors of Holy Ghost church every single morning. The teachers and staff knew my family and they treated me well because of it.

School was a thorn in my side even with the good treatment and respect. I struggled with my grades, especially in math. I just couldn't make my brain understand how to do the lessons. I hated math. I *still* hate math. The numbers and equations refused to connect in my mind. This was especially difficult because my father put such a high emphasis on grades. I remember often feeling like I was failing him. I was afraid to tell him I was struggling because I didn't want to add weight to his already heavy burden; mostly, I just didn't want to disappoint my father. I knew he expected me to do well, but I just couldn't reach the impossibly high bar he had set for me.

Now, when I talk to my father about those years, he doesn't recall that I struggled in school. His recollection was that I was a good student, and that I did very well in school. We have two completely different recollections about this part of my young life. His is likely about my behavior in school. It is true that I was a good kid. I didn't get into trouble at school. I did what was expected of me and followed the rules. I was never a problem for my teachers. I was well-mannered and well-behaved, and I got along well with my classmates, at least for the most part. I suppose this felt like a great accomplishment given what we had been through.

I could have easily gone in the other direction; causing trouble, fighting, disrespecting my teachers and peers. But my father's disciplined expectations at home taught me what was expected of me and my behavior, both at home and in public. There was no leeway. I was expected to behave, and I didn't dare step outside the boundaries that my father built. I was acutely aware that I was an extension of my father and his standing and reputation in our community. Anything I did would reflect on him. I knew well enough not to do anything that would tarnish my father's hard work at building a solid reputation.

So, I behaved, and I did what was expected of me. I never stepped out of line. I just couldn't fully connect while at school. I was easily distracted, and the lessons were often difficult for me to follow. It was all a bit over my head, especially math. Always math.

Perhaps my inability to retain the material and connect the dots was an outward expression of what was going on inside. It is hard to know. I certainly don't think that losing my mother had zero impact on my ability to learn and enjoy life at school. Even if it wasn't outwardly obvious to others—even my father–I was still grieving her loss and learning to live life without her. I cannot imagine any area of my life *not* being affected by the loss of my mother. This kind of grief and sorrow is not something you can compartmentalize and go about your life with no fall-out, especially not as a child. The effects spill out and over into everything. It does not have to look like bad behavior, getting in trouble, or chaos. It can be more subtle, like struggling in math. As a young kid, doing well in school is a huge part of life. It is sort of the only thing you have to worry about.

Maybe this was me subconsciously throwing up a red flag, saying *everything is not okay with me*. I know a lot of teachers who say that you can tell what is going on in a kid's home life from what is going on with them at school. This seems totally reasonable to me. As a man looking back, I can see this as a very definite possibility. I could not articulate or express the depths of my feelings. I don't think I could even understand the depths of my feelings, let alone articulate or express them. Something had to give, and that something was math.

I wonder what may have happened if this same situation was playing out today? Much more is known about childhood loss and childhood post-traumatic stress disorder. The response to my consistent failing grades in math may have been met with a more head-on approach. I can assume that more interventions would be put in place, and I would have received more support.

Everyone was showing up for me in the best ways they knew how. I do not fault anyone for lack of care or effort. The problem was no one had been through this *exact* situation. It was completely uncharted territory, and everyone was figuring it out as they went along, walking on eggshells so as not to release something from inside of me that would make the situation even harder.

My father recalls hiring a tutor to help me at different intervals over the years. The tutor did not help much, and unfortunately, I still could not make the grades and math was still a puzzle that I could not solve no matter how hard I tried. I venture to say this is not the type of help I needed. I needed therapy, a consistent time to talk through my feelings with a third party whom my own emotions could not hurt.

I needed a compassionate witness.

This comes up time and time again as I think about life. I needed someone who would encourage me to talk; someone who would help carry some of my pain without any ounce of judgment or trying to *fix it*. I needed someone to just sit with me and help me to see that everything would be okay. The fourth grade Reggie, the fifth grade Reggie, and the sixth grade Reggie was longing for and needed a compassionate witness. Instead, I managed the best I knew how.

When report card time came, I would begin to feel anxious and nervous. I knew my math grade would be failing, especially in the middle years—fourth, fifth, and sixth grade—as the material became more involved and more challenging. I already did not possess a solid math foundation, so when we began learning long division, fractions, and pre-algebra, I could not keep up.

I am sweating a bit now as I write this.

I had a lot of anxiety surrounding my inability to learn math. To this day, my father does not know —or maybe he did know and looked the other way—but I did a lot of forging and grade changing on my report cards. I would find a document with my father's signature and carefully trace it in the parent signature section. I wonder if maybe even my teachers knew. If this were happening with a high-risk student today, I am certain that there would be concerned phone calls, parent meetings, and well-laid plans to help me do better. I don't recall any of these interventions taking place.

Not only would I forge my father's signature, but I also changed the F's into A's in math. The teachers back then made their F's lowercase: f. I would carefully continue the rounded top of the f all the way down to the bottom and turn it into an A. Imagine a capital A with a rounded instead of a pointed top. I don't know how I got away with this for so long, which is why I wonder if everyone knew exactly what was going on and I was getting some sort of *dead mother pass*.

I guess that's the thing about red flags; they are much clearer in hindsight. Everyone was just doing their best, me included.

ICEE

A s I got to be a bit older—ten to twelve—my father began leaving me home alone when he went to work at night. It was never for long periods of time, and I was old enough to take care of myself. He knew that I would be perfectly fine, otherwise he would never have left me alone. My father always made sure I was covered, and I am sure that he also gave a heads-up to our neighbor Ms. Dorothy to keep an eye on me as well.

When he was gone, I would do normal adolescent boy things, like play video games, and eat snacks. I was never allowed to leave the house when he was gone at night. This was a set boundary that I did not dare cross. Truth be told, this was not a boundary that I even cared to challenge. I didn't love being home alone, especially at night, so there was no way I was going to leave the safety of our house.

It was around this time that my father and I began what I call our *silent exchanges*. A lot went unspoken between us during the first few years after my mother's death, but there was an understanding between us. We did not have to talk through much to understand one another. It was just our way. Looking back, I wish we had both said more out loud. We were both doing our best to survive, and long conversations about our feelings did not fit into our mode of survival.

Something that I would do almost nightly when my father was gone was page him. There were no cell phones back then, so

the easiest and fastest way to get in touch with him was by pag-
ing him. I would wait until later into the night, typically when
I would start to get anxious and nervous about whether he was
going to come home. Most young boys wouldn't worry so much
about this. They may call if they were scared or hearing noises.
It was different for me. I worried about whether he would come
home. I feared the absolute worst possible scenario.

I had reason to worry. If my mother could go out and never
come home, surely this could just as easily happen to my father,
right? Statistically, this would be highly improbable; but my
mind and heart didn't care about statistics and probability. To
me, it was a very real possibility that one night, he just wouldn't
come home. Most kids do not sit around thinking about their
parent dying, or just never coming home. Most kids at this age
are busy being kids. They are self-absorbed and do not typically
think of much outside of themselves. *That* is a *normal* childhood.
On those nights when my father was gone, I should have been
busy being a kid.

I would beep my father, and then wait anxiously for him to
call me back. The phone would ring . . .

"Hello"

"Lil' Reggie, it's me . . . is everything alright?"

"Yeah, everything's fine. I was just calling to see if you could
bring me home an Icee."

"Okay, yeah. I'll bring you home an Icee, son."

We would end our short call and I would breathe a sigh of
relief. My father was okay, and he was coming home.

He never brought me an Icee.

Those calls were never about the Icee, and we both knew it. Some nights it was an Icee, or a burger and fries, and some nights it was a pack of gum from the corner store. He always said, "Okay, Lil' Reggie, okay." But, he never came home with any of my requests. He knew my hidden request was for him to simply *come home*.

Fear was a big part of my childhood. Though it was not visible and overbearing, I still lived a lot of my childhood in fear. I always feared that one day my dad just wouldn't come home; that either something terrible would happen to him, or that one day he would decide that raising me as a single father along with the weight of loss and his own grief was too much to bear. I was always waiting for the other shoe to drop. Surely it would, right? One day it would all come crashing down again, right?

The worst possible thing had already happened to me, but I was sure the other shoe would drop at any moment. This is the thinking of a child who has been through trauma. I lived in constant fear. This changes a kid; steals his innocence. My father and I never spoke about the nights I paged him. It was one of our silent exchanges; just another part of how we lived our lives. We never spoke about our fears out loud, but I am sure he had his own worst-case scenario sitting in the back of his mind. I am sure he lived a lot like me, waiting for the other shoe to drop.

Neither of us had the emotional language to express what we were going through, or how we were feeling, so there was no reason to talk about it. He knew very well that when I paged him, I was calling to check on him. My page was the silent cue for him to get on home as soon as he could. Those calls told him that I had been alone long enough, and I needed him to come home. And he always did. I would hear his car pull up in the carport and breathe a deep sigh of relief.

He was home. All was right with the world in that moment.

If I am being totally honest, I still do this routine of checking in when my wife is out, or away from home. It was more pronounced early in our dating life and within the first few years of marriage. I never asked her for an Icee or a pack of gum, but I would ask where she was, and what time she planned to head home. I suppose this is part habit and part trauma response. I am fiercely protective of my family, so those calls are me making sure that *everyone is okay at all times*. As I write the words everyone is okay at all times, I realize what a heavy burden this is for someone to carry. Yet, I shoulder it. I don't consciously feel the weight of it, it is simply something that I do, an extension of survival mode.

I don't know if I will ever stop making check-in calls, or if I will ever trust that everyone is okay. I wonder how this will look like as my son grows older. I wonder if my fear and anxiety will smother him. I know that most parents deal with this, so circumstances dictate that I will struggle more than the average father. As my son gets older and gains more independence, I will have to decide if I am okay existing within this sphere of anxiety, or if I want to live trusting that he will be okay.

It is a constant struggle to decide what parts of my past to leave behind, and which of them to carry forward into my present life. Sometimes I don't even realize that I am operating out of fear, or that I live my life in survival mode. Sometimes it takes someone from the outside looking in to help me recognize my coping mechanisms and survival behaviors. I don't want to raise my son to spend his life in survival mode. I want him to live a limitless and abundant life without fear, thriving rather than merely surviving.

I realize that through my process of self-reflection and self-awareness, that I must change in order to build a different life for my family—for my son. How does one do such a thing? How does one change something that is so ingrained in their subconscious? I do not yet have the answers, but asking the questions and writing this book are both huge steps for me. I am taking baby steps, but I am walking. Self-transformation is difficult. It is a slow process of unlearning old habits and behaviors. It requires rewriting stories that we have told ourselves for years, even decades. The tapes we play on repeat within our heads need to be paused, and we must record new stories.

For decades my tapes have told me that the world is unsafe. They instill fear and anxiety on an endless loop from which there is no escape. In some instances, their stories keep me and others safe. It is good to be aware as you move through the world, attuned to things around you that may cause harm. However, for those who have experienced trauma, there is no distinction between safety and survival. The mind of a trauma survivor interprets *everything* as unsafe. The fight or flight response kicks in and we lose our ability to think rationally through our circumstances. This pattern of thought and behavior elicits a great deal of avoidance. It is easier to avoid situations than to fight through them.

Avoidance is a coping mechanism, another survival tool in the already crowded tool belt. It is easier to avoid the thing that *may* cause us discomfort or pain, rather than take the leap and hope for the best. It is easier for me to not put myself out there than it is to take a chance and see what happens. Avoidance is one of my favorite tools. It keeps me safe. It keeps my family safe. I stay in *control* (another tool in my belt), but I am beginning to realize that this is no way to live. While the boundaries I set and the walls I build may keep me and my family safe, they also keep us from fully experiencing the abundance of joy that life can bring.

I am sick of boundaries and walls. I am tired of the limitations I place on my own life and the lives of my family. I want to live fully and unafraid. I want the peace and confidence of knowing that no matter what happens *everyone will be okay*.

My spirit is stirring as I write this because I know that an abundant life is just within my grasp. I have done the work, digging up the old thinking and identifying the problem. Now I must do the work on rewiring my thinking. There is a thrill to it because I feel hope; I see the possibility of a better way of living. I can imagine a feeling of peace and the absence of fear, and I long for it.

I am claiming this new life in advance. I see the light at the end of the tunnel. It is bright, and draws me in. And so, I begin. One foot in front of the other. Every single day I will decide that *today,* I will look for the light. I will move away from fear and toward the bright light of peace and joy.

PAINTING THE VAULT

My father and I would tend to my mother's gravesite on a specific day, every summer. He called our yearly ritual *painting the vault*. I would know the time had come when he began gathering supplies. I can still hear him shaking the small can of gold paint, the lead ball bouncing off the sides of the aluminum can.

Click-clack-Click-clack-Click-clack.

My father would wake me early in the morning so we could beat the heat of the day. He would dress head to toe and would tell me to do the same: Jeans, long sleeved shirt, hat, and no exposed skin. He would carefully gather all the supplies, a quiet sort of ritual.

These visits to my mother's gravesite were not about sitting or reflecting, they were about working. This was my father's way of showing his continued love and respect for my mother. We would start working right away, with no time for words or feelings. My father would begin cleaning the site, making it worthy of my mother. He would begin pulling weeds, still wet with the morning dew that would soon burn away in the brutal heat of the sun. He would meticulously sand the areas of chipped paint on the vault and carefully wipe it clean. After sanding and cleaning, he would ready the vault for a fresh coat of paint, applying a layer of primer to cut down on mold and chipping. After the primer dried, he would begin re-painting the vault in bright gold.

By this time, the sun would be fully in the sky, bearing down on us as we labored. When I grew older, my father began handing some of the harder work over to me. I had watched him perform this ritual all my life, so I knew exactly what to do. I knew his standards, so I worked slowly, carefully, meticulously, just as he had.

I remember these days vividly. The summer sun and smothering Louisiana heat were brutal, especially since we were clothed head to toe. There was no shade in the graveyard, and sweat poured down my face and back, pooling behind my knees. I never understood why my father didn't schedule this ritual during the spring or fall. Perhaps this was another lesson or method of training for me. We would work, regardless of the weather or our personal comfort, until it was perfect.

We honored my mother this way year after year, in the blazing hot Louisiana heat.

This ritual was a tangible way for my father to care for my mother, an outward expression of his love and dedication to her. He wanted me to see this kind of love and commitment with my own eyes. He wanted me to understand the importance of making sure her gravesite was beautifully maintained.

This was much more than a layer of fresh paint and flowers. The ritual of painting the vault was deeper than that. This was an act of devotion and reverence for my mother. It was an act of total selflessness, with no reward other than the feeling of pride and love we felt after making my mother's final resting place as beautiful as she was. This is quite a lesson for a young boy. It taught me discipline and commitment to a cause greater than myself. We did not perform the work for the recognition of our family or our peers; we did it from a deep place of nurturing care. Some of the lessons of this sacrifice were lost on me at the time; but, looking back, I now see that my father's true motives were to honor my mother.

He could have easily accepted the help of the graveyard employees; they did a fairly decent job of keeping everything well maintained. But that was never good enough for my father. *Fairly decent* did not live up to his standards or expectations, especially when it came to my mother. Her final resting place must be absolutely perfect, and he knew he was the only person in the whole world who could do it exactly right.

He would never trust this task of love to anyone else. Not even to me.

Sometimes when we were done, we would sit for a while. I would cry, and he would comfort me with an arm around my shoulders, pulling me into a side hug. We would often sit there for hours, the sun still beating mercilessly on our faces and sweat running in small rivers down our backs and cheeks.

I don't recall exactly when we stopped painting the vault. It must have been around the time that I left home. I always wondered if my dad kept the ritual going, buying the paint, and collecting all the materials the night before.

I've never asked him.

Maybe the ritual was just for me.

YOU KNOW I LOVE YOU

I have always struggled with understanding my father's way of showing love. It was not soft or affectionate, like the love of a mother. He chose to express love through actions rather than words. My father's love was his unfailing presence, and the fact that he chose to stay when it would have been so easy to give up and go.

Raising a son as a single father was surely a challenge. But he did it. He woke up every single day and did what needed to be done—and did it well. My father was a *good* father. I knew that he loved me; but, if I am being completely honest, my father was not an easy man to please. He could be extremely hard on me. He was never abusive—emotionally, verbally, or physically—he just had extremely high expectations where I was concerned. Perhaps his Marine Corps background was to blame, as he could be a bit of a drill sergeant at times. For the most part, I think he was hard on me because he was trying to prepare me for the world; to be successful. If he prepared me, he knew I would be okay.

Being this involved with your son takes a great deal of sacrifice and dedication, and he never wavered. I consider his sacrifices a great act of love.

We developed our own way of communicating and living with one another that was uniquely ours, shaped and molded by our circumstances. My father had a very specific way of acting and interacting in the world, as well as a unique and specific way of communicating, both with others and with me. Our communication was directly influenced and molded by our personal baggage and shared circumstances.

Even though I was so young, I, too, had my ways of communicating. I did not have years of experience interacting with the world like my father did, but my personality and ways of relating to others reflected how my father and I communicated at home. When I say *communicated*, I am not just talking about how we spoke with one another. I refer to how we lived, and how our lives mingled together under the roof of our little home. There is a lot that goes on in a relationship like ours. We were father and son; we were also friends, and companions. We counted on one another—a lot.

I struggle to articulate the depth of our relationship in the early years. One thing that always stood out to me was my father's way of telling me that he loved me. This may seem trivial, but it was an aspect of our communication that always hurt a little as I was growing up. I get emotional even now as a grown man when I think about it.

When I was growing up, my father never said the words *I love you*.

It seems even more trivial as I write this. I have shared the myriad ways that my father showed up for me every single day, showing his love in numerous ways without ever wavering in his commitment to me. He was, and still is, a solid source of real love in my life.

But he never said those three simple but complicated words: *I love you*.

He would say it in roundabout ways, like, *you know I love you*; but he never actually uttered the simple phrase *I love you*. The roundabout ways did not reach the deep need in me to hear these words. I know it is complicated, and I struggle to explain it. In saying the phrase, *you know I love you*, my father somehow put pressure on me, instead of just allowing me to hear and internalize the straightforward *I love you*. The lack of the "I" makes the sentence seem non-committal, too casual for the love from a father to a son.

You know I love you.

Do I know? This implies that I *should* know. But how do I know you love me if you never actually tell me that you love me? This passive verbal expression of love can cause questioning and doubt in the mind of a child. It feels conditional, even non-committal, like at any moment he would just stop saying it. Of course, I knew my father loved me, even if I didn't understand his way of expressing it in words. But I was a kid and was already processing so much. I was still forming my thoughts and beliefs, figuring out what I knew.

We do not get to a place of truly knowing things until we are older and have lived much more life. I don't think I could receive the love my father was offering through the roundabout. I very much needed and longed for a direct expression of love, such as the words "I love you." I needed to know and to feel like he really did love me and meant those words with all his heart, and that no matter what may happen, he would always love me.

The words I love you are powerful, perhaps the most powerful in the English language. Together they hold immeasurable weight and meaning. There are numerous ways of saying I love you that are far less powerful. The short-cut version, or round-abouts, do not hit us in the same way. They do not feed our deep need to be loved, and to be told directly that we are loved.

Love ya.

Love you.

These are just a couple examples of the common short-cuts we use, especially now that so much of our communication occurs via text messaging. These phrases are casual, and do not hold the same weight as fully saying "*I love you.*"

It just is not the same.

One simple vowel—*I*—changes the whole meaning. The use of the word *I* indicates the person recognizes and feels the love within themselves, and they understand that it is not some sort of fleeting emotion. They feel this love deep within themselves. There is no implied pressure on the person accepting the love. It implies that the person saying it has thought about it and is willing to put their whole selves out there.

The words *I love you* when expressed with sincerity is a pure gift, with zero strings attached. It is active, direct, and extremely personal. I am sure there were numerous reasons why my father could not say the words *I love you*; in fact, I am almost certain he learned some of this from his own father, and his father before him. Men do not typically feel as comfortable expressing their love in words. It is much easier for them to show it in action and deed. It can also be cultural, learned from generations of family dynamics. If you were not directly told *I love you* as a child, it is likely that you will adopt the same roundabout way of expressing love yourself.

It's also possible that my father was simply afraid to say *I love you*. Saying these words means putting your whole heart on the line, wearing your heart on your sleeve. It is risky, and sometimes you get hurt when you feel this deeply. Perhaps he too was dealing with the fear of more loss. Maybe *I love you* was just too scary for him. I struggled with my fear that one night he just wouldn't come home, so it stands to reason that he was working through similar struggles surrounding me. It is safer to hold a bit back and keep your love close to your chest. Extending it means you may get hurt, and perhaps the thought of more hurt was simply paralyzing.

As a kid who had already been through so much, I needed my father to give me his whole heart. I needed the expression of love to be deep and wide, active, and personal. I needed to be the recipient of this precious gift. But I understand it all now. I can sympathize and empathize with what may have been keeping him from putting his whole heart on the line, and I have no ill will toward my father—zero. I see it clearly now, and I understand.

In June of 2019 my father is taken into custody by the Tangipahoa Parish police. He is an inmate in Tangipahoa Parish prison; however, we talk on the phone as often as possible. And for the first time in all my life my father ends our phone calls with the words "I love you."

Finally.

I don't know if this is because we are on the phone and it feels a bit safer to be more open and vulnerable, or if perhaps the thought of being behind bars forever has created a sense of urgency in him to say the things he never said. Either way, I am finally hearing the words that I have longed to hear. Hearing my father say these three simple words has brought a healing that I did not even know I needed. It is funny how three simple words can change everything.

I have learned a lot from reflecting on this specific part of my childhood. I want to say out loud all the things that need to be said to all the people I love. I want to practice being more open and vulnerable, telling my own son *I love you* so that this is his memory of how I expressed my love to him.

Again, hope. Hope always bats last. Hope always has the final say. Hope always wins.

What I was missing in my childhood is now restored. It may have taken the drastic and life altering circumstance of my father going to prison, but we now speak the words "I love you" freely and without fear. We give it, and we receive it—this soothing balm for both of our hearts.

Today, tell your people *I love you*. Tell them every day. Never hold back. Never let fear get in the way. Stop using the round-abouts, even if it is scary and you think you may get hurt. Say it anyway. When we come to the end of our lives, we will never regret having spoken our love.

LAB SCHOOL

After spending seven years at Holy Ghost School, my teachers and the administration made the decision to hold me back in the 6th grade. I continued to struggle in school despite the extra help of tutors. I still couldn't get a handle on things, especially math. School and I just did not add up.

I don't know why they chose the 6th grade, especially since I really cannot think of anything worse for a pre-teen. All my classmates would be moving ahead into the junior high years, and I would be stuck—alone—to do the whole year all over again.

I do not know why they didn't intervene earlier, perhaps in the third or fourth grade. Maybe they had been holding their breath, waiting, and hoping that things would settle down for me, and then somehow things at school would begin to click. Unfortunately, that did not happen, and I am not sure it ever would have.

I begged my father to move me to another school in town, specifically, the Lab School. I could not bear the thought of having to repeat the sixth grade at Holy Ghost. I knew a few kids from the neighborhood who attended the Lab School, and I had heard so many amazing stories about it. It was still so foreign to me that kids could enjoy going to school. I knew it must be different, and I had to see what all the hype was about.

I begged.

I pleaded.

Shockingly, my father conceded easily. I couldn't believe it. I had convinced my inconvincible father to allow me something that was important to *me*. I think he knew how desperately I needed the change—perhaps he did too.

Lab school was a turning point for me. It was vastly different from the tight walls and rigid boundaries of Holy Ghost. The classrooms were designed with open floor plans, and students moved about freely between classes. We were allowed to interact with students of all grades, building relationships with teachers and administrators outside of the traditional classroom. It was wide open, no unnecessary constraints, restrictions, or boundaries.

My eyes—and my world—opened wide, and I took it all in. This felt more like home than any other place in my life. The student body was diverse, and the teaching much more dynamic. For once in my life, I began to know what success felt like. This was life-changing for me in so many ways. I needed openness and freedom, and I began thriving rather than merely surviving.

School and I clicked. We added up.

Maybe this was what I needed all along—openness, freedom, and a taste of success. I needed to be surrounded by kids that lived in my neighborhood—kids that looked like me. Lab school was an awakening. I had been going through the motions, tethered to a short leash for far too long. I was ready to grow up and move on, and this new environment allowed me to do that.

The teen years are a time when kids begin to naturally separate from their parents. It is a rite of passage, and very much on target developmentally. Separation happens in order to prepare both parent and child for the inevitability of growing up and moving away. It is necessary for a healthy young adult to prepare for entering adulthood. I became my own person during these years, separate from my father. Feeling successful instilled me with confidence, and I began to feel at home in my own skin.

The absence of my mother no longer loomed over me as large as it once had. She was never far from my thoughts, but she began to move out of the forefront of my mind. I was a typical self-absorbed pre-teen. I wanted to hang out with my friends, talk to girls on the phone, and do all the things a typical junior high kid does. I was still living the same story, but I had turned the pages and entered a new chapter.

My mother had been gone for more years than I had known her. If she had been alive, I would have been naturally separating from her as well as from my father. Perhaps this is why her absence felt less palpable. I didn't need her love and encouragement in the same way I did as a young boy. I was beginning to see my own worth and value.

I begin formulating life-sized dreams for myself. I wanted to be an actor, and not just any kind of actor. I wanted to be wildly famous. I wanted to be on the main stage, the person whom everyone looked up to. This may seem like an odd dream for a boy like me, but I think it speaks volumes about what was happening in my life.

I was allowing myself to dream, finally seeing that things in my imagination were not impossibilities. The world and all it had to offer was opening itself up to me. If I had stayed at Holy Ghost, I would have remained behind the curve, struggling, surviving, unable to see and dream about my future. I would have remained tightly tethered to my father, too insecure in myself to separate.

At the Lab School we went on field trips, did real-life projects, and were given more responsibility. This led to more and more confidence and assurance that my life would be one of great abundance, rather than defined by loss. The magnitude of this hits me squarely in the chest even today. There are places, people, and institutions that breed survival; they are part of what makes the world turn. There are also places, people, and institutions that foster growth and success regardless of background or circumstance.

The Lab School was the latter of these two, encouraging growth and teaching me to thrive after so many years of standing still with clenched fists and fear in my eyes. I could finally move, my hands open to the possibilities that I never imagined were available to a boy like me. My academic world went from small, silent grey rooms with perfect rows of desks, to wide open spaces filled with color, conversations, books, and art.

I was coming home to myself.

I don't know where I would be today without the Lab School. This change came at just the right time to save my life. I mean this quite literally; it saved my life. It saved me from a life riddled with self-doubt, insecurity, and an unhealthy extended attachment to my father. I think it was three of the most formative years of my entire life.

I do not want to say that I had finally moved on. I don't know if one ever truly moves on, waking up on morning thinking *today is the day I'm moving on*. No, time just passes, and with every day, week, month, and year the piercing pain that once consumed me became less intense. The passing time combined with my new-found freedom allowed me the space to leave childhood and all that came with it behind. It gave me the permission I needed to step fully into my life for the very first time; to become a young man.

I would always carry the weight of my mother's loss, but now I could shoulder the weight of it without crumbling. Life began to take on a new meaning.

I am eternally grateful and humbled to have found this path at just the right time. It was a pivotal point in my life, needed more so than anyone could know. I visualize it like moving from the fetal position, barely able to breathe, to lying on my back with my arms confidently behind my head, staring straight up into the night sky. I smile at the endless possibilities before me. I am tired, but at last wide awake. Life began to matter. *I* began to matter. My starving spirit had been infused with endless hope. I was going to be okay.

Finally, I could breathe.

PART TWO

THE NOW

MOTHER'S DAY 2020

My father has been in Tangipahoa prison since June 23rd, 2019. As Mother's Day approaches, things have begun to weigh heavily on me, even more so in a year when the world is being rocked by the global pandemic, COVID-19. I talk to my father frequently, and he never seems too bothered by his current situation. I know that he would never want me to feel bad for him or worry about his well-being. But I do worry. Prison is prison. It is not a good place to be. Prison is awful.

You don't need to have a loved one or someone you know in prison to understand that the conditions and treatment of inmates are nothing short of inhumane. Even though my father seems content and at peace, conducting a sort of prison ministry with his Bible classes, I know what he is dealing with behind bars, and it isn't pretty. I worry about his health, safety, and over-all well-being. He is my father. I don't want to think of him being forced to endure these types of conditions while worrying about the threat of contracting a potentially fatal virus. You know they aren't taking the necessary precautions to ensure the health and wellness of the inmates, such as cleaning and sanitizing.

They don't give a shit.

In the prison system people are just numbers, their humanity stripped away the moment they walked through the doors. My father doesn't say much about the treatment he and the other inmates receive, but I do know that at one point in early 2020, they were only being given two small meals each day. They had a small breakfast around 5 a.m., and a cold, brown paper bag style lunch around 1 p.m. Do not imagine your breakfast—imagine *prison* breakfast. Lunch typically included nothing more than a sandwich. Again, don't imagine a sandwich that you would make for yourself or your kids; imagine a *prison* sandwich. After the sandwich, they would not eat another meal until the next morning at 5 a.m. That is nearly 16 hours without food unless you bought something from the commissary; but even that would be a small, insignificant snack.

Inhumane.

The lack of food is just one of the many things that weighed on me as I imagined him in prison. In the spring of 2020, my father told me that he and the other inmates had not been outdoors since the prior year, sometime in the fall or winter of 2019. They had not been allowed to see the light of day or feel the sun on their faces in months. They were given no explanation as to why they were no longer going outside, it simply *was*.

Can you imagine?

Even though it is prison, it's customary to allow inmates a specific amount of recreational time outdoors at least once a day. Some inmates choose to play basketball or run the perimeter of the yard for exercise. Some just sit and enjoy the warmth of the sunlight on their faces, breathing in the fresh air. This time allows them a brief respite from the stagnant conditions that they live with inside the prison walls. It is like a tiny bit of freedom, even if for only a short time. It is good for morale.

When that time is taken away, the effects begin to show themselves quickly. Everyone needs fresh air and sunlight, even inmates. Knowing that they have withheld this simple thing makes me angry, not just for my father, but for all the inmates. It is as if they are being punished beyond their sentences. Being outdoors makes a person feel connected to the world; withholding it further dehumanizes them. It is awful, and it isn't right. I know this happens in prisons everywhere, and many are much worse; but, thinking about it happening to my father was a burden so heavy that I could not shake it.

My father called me that spring and told me that the television in their cell unit was broken. He said that the inmates had been trying to get someone to fix it, but so far, no one had done so. There was some talk among the inmates about whether this was another form of punishment. The single television that they had to watch was just sitting there broken, with no plan for repairing it. My father said the inmates were asking their family members to call the prison and request that the television be repaired or replaced.

So, I called.

I stated my name, my father's name, and my concern over the broken television. I asked the representative nicely why it hadn't been fixed, inquired as to what needed to be done to make that happen, and expressed that my father really needed this small joy to help him get through the day while serving his time. The guy on the other end of the phone laughed.

"Are you seriously calling me about a broken TV?" His voice dripped sarcasm.

"Yes, sir. I am," I replied.

He laughed again. I could tell he was frustrated and annoyed, but I continued my inquiry. He responded again with sarcasm, making it clear that he cared little for the effect this was having on the inmates, *especially* my father. I could tell this was going nowhere.

What kind of person acts and speaks to another person this way without provocation? I was kind and respectful, expressing my concern through the proper channels. Would he be this sarcastic and flippant if the roles were reversed, and *his* father was being treated with a complete lack of compassion? I was beyond pissed. I was livid. I wasn't asking for much, just a little TV that worked. With hardly any food, no fresh air, and a broken TV, I knew that my father and the other inmates had no connection to the outside world, no chance for even a simple escape from their current conditions.

I asked my wife to call the prison. She approached the situation in the same way I had, with respect and kindness. She expressed her concerns and was met with the same lack of compassion. I don't recall if we spoke with the same person, but we both got the same response. We were left with the feeling that we were somehow being a bother, and that we were wasting their time.

Perhaps prison beats the humanity out of the people who work there as well. I cannot imagine responding to another person this way, even under similar circumstances. Yes, these men are inmates, but they are still *people*. Each one is someone's father, brother, or son. They are human beings. The phone calls gave me a taste of how inmates are treated—like animals. It is heart-breaking and inhumane. The prison system is broken.

All these things combined with the approaching Mother's Day began to sit on me like a ton of bricks. I couldn't imagine my father in there, hungry, desperate for fresh air, and without a TV to watch now and again. It overtook my thoughts, and I could no longer escape the images that my mind had created.

Reality struck, and everything came crashing down.

My father had been taken away from my childhood home and put behind bars for the vicious murder of my mother.

I get nauseous writing these words.

How is this my life?

How is this *his* life?

How did this happen?

Why is this happening?

Everything cracked open and spilled out, and I could no longer contain the harshness of my reality. I began to make a plan. I had to get my father out. I had to do everything within my power to bring him home. I am a young man with plenty of life left and time to recoup any money that I spent to get him released. I knew that if I didn't do everything I could—even if it involved huge financial risk and sacrifice—I wouldn't be able to live with myself.

If you don't know anything about bonding someone out of prison, here is your crash course: My father's bond was set at $250,000, which is an insane amount of money. Bond is the reason he was still in prison. When he first went to prison, I couldn't bail him out. I didn't have that kind of money. If I had that kind of money lying around, I would have gotten my father out long ago. The powers that be intentionally set bail this high to make getting out impossible. Not many people have hundreds of thousands of dollars on hand to bail someone out of prison.

But I had to get him out.

So, I found a way.

Here's how it works: You either have to put up a piece of un-mortgaged property worth equal to or more than the bond amount or hire a bail bondsman and pay their fee plus the bond percentage. In my case that fee was 12%. That's twelve percent of $250,000, or $30,000. Thirty thousand dollars that you do not get back regardless of the trial outcome. Innocent. Guilty. Hung jury. I'll never see that money again.

I sacrificed a great deal, but I am at peace with my decision. I no longer feel the heaviness of imagining my father hungry, longing to breathe fresh air into his lungs and feel the warmth of the sunshine on his face. He is home and will remain there with an ankle monitor until his trial.

As of now, my father's trial has been pushed back from June 2020 to December 2020 due to the COVID-19 crisis. My father has been assigned an amazing public defender. In a book about my mother's case entitled *Bayou Justice*, author H.L. Arledge describes this woman as "not your stereotypical public defender. She raises her hands when she talks, and often raises her voice when speaking to judges." She cares a great deal about her clients and has been especially involved with my father's case, always keeping us up-to-date and informed.

I am scheduled to be a witness at my father's trial, so I have limited access to the full discovery files. I will have to wait and hear the evidence in real time, as it is being presented by the prosecution and the defense. I would be lying if I said I wasn't anxious about the trial, especially about testifying. I know that I can handle myself, but cross-examination can be notoriously vicious. They will try to get me to turn on my father, much like the day of the interrogation when they tried to separate us. They will do everything they can to discredit me, thereby discrediting my father. I think this would cause anyone a great deal of fear and anxiety, but I will show up for my father, and my mother. I will tell the whole truth. I can only hope the truth prevails and justice is served.

I have never thought that my father was capable of killing my mother. Never. If you were given the opportunity to know my father better, I am certain you would feel the same. I know people are capable of all sorts of terrible things, and that my father is far from perfect—we all are. But he is not a murderer. He loved and respected my mother. They were friends and a good team. There is just no possible way that he killed his best friend and the mother of his boy.

At his trial, there will be a group of prosecutors who don't know my father, and who will be hell-bent on making twelve jurors believe without a doubt that he killed my mother. They will paint him as a person capable of taking my mother's life. This is their job, I suppose, but I hold out hope; hope that the truth will be revealed and that my father's character will shine through. I hope for doubt to emerge in the evidence and within the minds of the 12 jurors. I realize that doubt is a strange thing to hope for, but, then again, this entire situation is strange and surreal.

I don't know how this is my life, and now suddenly my father's life. Thirty-three years have passed, and nothing—absolutely nothing—emerged. More than three solid decades of nothing, and now the prosecution is sure they have found her killer. And they are sure it is my father.

My father ran for public office in the years after my mother's death. If there was ever a time for salacious information to emerge, it would be during a political campaign. But nothing. How could they not have known then what they know now? How can they be so sure *now*? None of it makes any sense. It feels arbitrary, out of nowhere. It feels like it is about much more than just finding out who took my mother's life.

This is an election year, and the district attorney is up for re-election. It would be great for him to say that he helped solve a three-decade old cold case. I suppose this would make his constituents feel safer and paint him in a positive light for voters. Politics can be ugly and heartless. Many politicians—not all, but many—are willing to sacrifice the lives of others to build their reputations and climb the political ladder. It is ugly and altogether unjust, but it happens all the time.

In addition to the complexity of politics, we are in the Deep South. If you live here and you are Black, you know where I am going with this. If you live here and you are White, I hope you see the truth and are an advocate and an ally for your friends and neighbors of color. I won't linger on this point for long as this could—and should—be its own separate book; but I would be remiss if I did not highlight the fact that this is a large part of what is happening with my father.

Louisiana is light years behind other states when it comes to politics, policing, and the criminal justice system. The fact that my father is a Black man surely weighs into the equation. Sadly, many in the South still criminalize Black men for no reason other than the color of their skin. If my father were a White man, I wager we would not be going through this at all. My mother's case would have been closed 33 years ago, never to be looked at again.

Saying that this is a lot to process and an extremely heavy weight to carry is the understatement of the century. My father's arrest, his time in prison, and the upcoming trial have elicited so many complex layers of emotion within me. This has been the most difficult time of my life. I have struggled to understand the meaning of it more over the past two years than I have in my entire lifetime. These two years have been the most intense, gut-wrenching, heart-breaking of my life. The fact that I have no say in what the outcome will be has turned me once again into that six-year-old boy. My life is not my own, and I am right back at the beginning with a whole life of heartache ahead of me.

I am tired, sad, and angry. I am confused, and even afraid. I feel alone, as my deepest fears have come back to pay me an unwanted visit. How is this my life? I don't want this life. I had moved on. I had not fully healed, but I had moved on.

Yet here I am.

Again.

LIMITS

For me, limits come in all shapes and sizes.

Limits are like little safety nets that I put up all around my life so that I never have to feel the pain of falling. Up to now, this has been an effective coping mechanism, and these safety nets have served me well. They have allowed me to stay afloat, continue surviving and build a life. My self-imposed guardrails have allowed me to become successful in my career. I excel in my work, and I am confident and highly effective at what I do. I have reached great potential.

My limiting behaviors are least prevalent in my work life. I often wonder what more I could do if these limiting behaviors were never a part of my life at all. Would I be even *more* successful? Would I be at the top of my field, a leader, even the person in charge? Would I have fulfilled my dream of becoming an actor? Would I be changing the lives of others in powerful and meaningful ways?

It is impossible to know.

My limiting behaviors show up most undeniably in my personal life, and I am just beginning to see the patterns I have created. I have begun processing and dismantling these self-limiting thoughts and behaviors. Limiting behaviors are an extension of survival mode. As I have said before, survival mode protects me from the pain and suffering associated with going too deep or feeling too much. I believe this is common, even for people who have not experienced great trauma. It is natural to seek to protect ourselves from the possibility of heartbreak. The more pain we have felt, the more limited and imprisoned we are by the walls we build to protect ourselves.

My limits—or walls—are most prevalent in my home life. Please understand that I am happily married, and I love my wife dearly. I love being a father, and our son is one of the great loves in my life. But this is where things get tricky, because all this love, affection, and connection feels a little bit unsafe. What if I lose them? What if one day they just don't come home? This has happened before, so I know it is a real possibility, which makes it a rational fear. For most people, these thoughts are fleeting; but, for me, this is a very real and present fear.

In my mind, I rationalize the possibility of my wife leaving one day and never coming home. Even worse, she could leave one day with our only son and never come home. The thought of this happening makes my stomach churn, and my heart race. I cannot lose them.

This is why I set up limits and safety nets. I built emotional walls to prevent the unthinkable pain from happening. The process was subtle, almost unconscious. I believe it was my subconscious trying to protect me. Outwardly, the walls are not obvious. I am not sitting in a physical fortress where nothing can touch me. It is way more subtle, like an inability to fully connect or be fully present in my home life and with the people I love the most.

It is confusing and frustrating and difficult for others to understand. I withhold a lot. I don't give of myself fully when it comes to emotional connections. I struggle with making intimate connections because I am still in survival mode, desperately afraid of more loss in my life. I hate all of this. My wife hates it. I fear that if I don't find a way to heal, my son and our future children will hate it as well.

I try to explain that the walls have nothing to do with my wife or son. This is all me. I have lived this way for so long that I don't know any other way to exist. I want so badly to connect and form relationships with the people that matter in my life; but I still have a great deal of healing and unlearning to do. I am committed to the work. I know it will be a difficult process, but I no longer want to live in this space. I am sick of disconnecting, numbing out, or hovering over my own life. I want to be fully present and truly alive in my life. I want to love my wife without hesitation and raise my son as a father who never holds back his love out of fear.

I think I overcompensate at work because of the disconnect I feel in my personal life. Work is safer because the people that I love are not directly involved. If I fail on a project or don't perform my best, I can blame myself and no one gets hurt. This is why I have been able to excel in my career. My childhood wounds don't manifest themselves at work. If anything, my wounds make me work harder. Work is a safe place to get lost in. I can shut out all the inner noise and completely immerse myself in the task at hand.

I love my life and my family. I want to love them more fully and deeply, without an ounce of hesitation. I want to live without limits, allowing myself to feel deep joy and connection without my mind whispering thoughts of loss.

You better not feel too much joy because something could come along and snatch it all away.

Oh, you better not feel that deeply. You are liable to get hurt . . . ."

These whispers are not lies. Everything *could* be snatched away, and I could be deeply hurt. The whispers are emotional dysfunction sneaking in, stealing my joy like a thief in the night. The boundaries I have built keep me from sharing all that I am, and from receiving all that others have to give me. The effect is two-fold in my ability and capacity to give love and connect with others and feel my feelings, as well as my ability and capacity to receive love and connect with others and share feelings on the deepest levels.

I am tired of treading water.

I am tired of living on the surface.

I no longer want to live this way.

Writing this book and sharing my story is part of the commitment to myself to do the hard work and unlearn boundary-building. I am taking a chance. It is risky to put your whole life down on paper; but, as I see it, I have no choice. I can either stay exactly where I am today—not growing or moving forward—or I can decide to move. I know well enough that if I choose the former my life will not have the depth and meaning that I so desire.

I wrote early on that though there is much pain in my story, but there is also great hope. This is the hope, the hope of change. The hope of healing and restoration, of a more abundant life full of deep connections with the people I love. There is so much hope. I feel it now as I write these words.

Truth be told, there is *only* hope. I refuse to go backward, so the only choice I have is to move forward. I can see the change. I can imagine and visualize what my life will be like as I begin to dismantle the walls around myself. It is exciting to uncover something about yourself and the way you are living and to decide that it is no longer working. It is both exciting and hopeful that we can decide today to do things differently and make our lives even better than they already are. I have made that choice.

This book is my dismantling. With every word a part of the wall crumbles. This is what happens when we expose our deep hurts to the light. They cannot survive in the light. They can no longer hold us hostage.

I feel the first signs of freedom, and the light ahead is bright.

"THE POST"

While writing this book, I have spent countless hours reflecting on my early childhood and teen years. Hindsight can be a gift, but it can also send you into a tailspin when you discover that the things you thought were true were far from it.

I think we all romanticize our childhoods. It is hard to acknowledge and accept the painful parts or reconcile that things were not perfect. It is even harder when we begin to see our parents—in my case, my father—as human beings, possessing all the flaws and scars we allow other people but rarely accept in the people we love the most.

My life on Apple Street was far from perfect.

I call it "The Post" because it was lacking so many of the things that make a house a home. Most importantly, it was lacking a mother—my mother. This made all the difference and changed everything in so many ways. Her murder sucked the life out of our little home. It went from *Home* to *The Post* in a single day.

When I think about that house now, it is just that—a house. It is where I went to eat, study, sleep, and do all the mundane things we do to survive. It is four walls and a roof over my head. It provided cover, but it lacked the safety and security which would have allowed me to move past survival into living and thriving. It was not a safe place to land.

I internalized this and allowed it to grow roots within myself, far-reaching and deep. I had no safe place. I began to see the world as unsafe, unstable, and unpredictable. Everything was out of my control. The Post became a symbol for what was happening to me on the inside. I did not feel at home within my own body. I was a stranger to myself then, and still am today. I never learned to trust myself, or others. People come and go. Experiences and circumstances can tear your heart out and break it into a million tiny pieces, over and over again. I am unsafe. The world is unsafe.

What is one to do when there is no soft landing space? Constant hustle. Kick the can. Keep it moving. This is what I did then and continue to do today. Idle time is not my friend. My mind races as I attempt to put the pieces of the puzzle together, but this puzzle has too many missing pieces. I stay busy. I hustle. I keep things moving. But I can only outrun myself for so long before my legs get tired. I am slowing down, and I feel like the race is coming to an end. I cannot run any longer. I don't want to, and I shouldn't have to. I deserve more. I want more. I need more.

As I have said before, my father could be a very hard man to live with. The bar he set was high and his expectations were often unreachable, many times making me feel like I was failing him. This created an unhealthy dynamic between us: Me always trying to please him and him, and him never allowing me to feel the reward of meeting his expectations. Nothing I did was ever good enough. Just when I thought I had reached the top, he would move the bar higher, or change the rules. I was not met with anger or disappointment; rather, I was given nothing at all. No reaction. No affirmation that I had done a good job or failed miserably. Indifference. Apathy. Silence. I don't know what is worse, anger or apathy. Disappointment or indifference.

This created the internal landscape for how I viewed myself, and it influenced my self-worth and how I navigated the world around me. It created in me a need and an endless drive to always be working—always be doing and striving. I needed to keep trying to meet my father's expectations, and I was never going to get there unless I kept hustling.

To him, this was building me up, giving me the tools necessary for survival. To me, it was slowly breaking me down, building self-doubt and a feeling that I would always fall just below the mark. I believe that his intentions were good, and I am sure that he meant no real harm. He knew the world and what it would take for me to not only survive but to find success. But he required a lot of me and expected more than I could ever offer.

It was a nonstop exhausting hustle.

A young boy can only handle so much of this. There were countless nights that I cried; out loud at first, then eventually silently to myself as he forced me to write meaningless sentences in an attempt to perfect my penmanship or read aloud to improve my reading skills. I just wanted to be a boy with space to grow and make mistakes. I wanted to rest. I wanted more than my father could give. I just wanted to *be*.

He knew no other way.

I wanted and deeply needed him to love me for who I *was*, and not for what I was able to do. I felt like I was always performing, trying to win his love and approval like a puppet on a string, an actor on a stage, or a hamster in an endlessly dizzying wheel. At best I was given "You know I love you." You already know what kind of a mind-fuck this was for me.

There was no winning with my father, only more hustling, more performing, more trying to gain approval. There was no nurturing, no room to make mistakes, and no grace. I didn't need to write more sentences or recite more lines from the Sunday paper. I needed my father to look me in the eyes and tell me that I was deeply loved and accepted for exactly who I was. I never got this, and because of that I still long for and seek his unconditional love and approval. All of this does something to a child, a young adult, and even a grown man.

I am just now beginning to unravel this mystery, and it is not pretty. It is not tidy. I am acutely aware that by writing this book I risk upsetting my father, dismantling, or even destroying his perception of our relationship growing up side by side.

But it is the truth.

It is *my* truth.

And it must be told.

The truth must exist somewhere outside of my own brain and heart. It is too big and too heavy. It is all-consuming, and I can no longer contain it. I do not write this book to hurt anyone or place blame, but to forever free myself from decades of believing I only had value if I was *doing* and doing *right*. It still has a tight grip on me, but I am beginning to believe that I have self-worth just as I am, and not because of what I have done or what I will do in the future. Being a perfectionist is a common trauma response.

We expect only the very best from ourselves and seek to control every tiny detail of our lives.

I have so much to unlearn, and so many new beliefs to accept and put into practice.

I have worth simply because of *who I am*. Unlearning and unraveling three decades of performance-based self-worth is one of the most challenging endeavors I have ever set out to do. Doubt creeps in, and negative self-talk becomes loud and convincing. Old habits are hard to break. I know if my mother had been there, she would have softened this side of my father. Perhaps he would have been a different kind of father without the weight of her absence bearing down on him. They would have balanced each other out. His expectations coupled with her unconditional love would have shaped me into an entirely different man than who I am today.

My mother would have celebrated my efforts and rewarded even my tiniest accomplishments. She would have been the opposite of indifference and apathy. She would have been the epitome of acceptance and acknowledgment. Her bar would have been high but movable so I would be able to reach it, and she would have honored my every effort. I would have known that she would accept me whether I lived up to them or not. My mother would have filled our house with unconditional love. In this, I would have learned the lessons and gained the confidence that comes from being noticed, acknowledged, and loved no matter what. There would have been less hustle and more room to just breathe: To just be.

I would have been loved for just *being*.

FIERCE INDEPENDENCE AND
TRAUMA RESPONSES

If you had told me back in my Holy Ghost School days when me and school didn't add up that I would end up going to college, I would have said you were absolutely crazy. But here I was, a high school graduate on the brink of setting out on my own. I felt all the excitement and possibilities that a young man feels when it is time for him to step fully into manhood. If you had told the little boy in the interrogation room trying desperately to get closer to his father that one day he would be strong enough to stand on his own, I wouldn't have believed you.

That is the thing about time and growing up. Scared little boys become confident young men, and going off to school comes at just the right time.

I was so ready for the next chapter in my life.

When your house doesn't feel like a home, and it isn't a safe place to be your true self, it is easy to leave. My father tried hard—I know he did. He tried to make that little house on Apple Street as much a home as he could, but it never quite felt that way to me. There were too many missing pieces; my mother being the most obvious. That house was and will always be "The Post," a place I went to eat and sleep.

When the time came for me to go to college, I couldn't wait to get the hell out of there. Even though I attended a local college close to home, I insisted on living on campus. It was time for me to be on my own and learn to be me—to breathe. My father called it "living college." And live I did.

I had a steady girlfriend at the time, and I was enjoying my new freedom. I spent most of my nights at her place, but I also had a place of my own when I needed or wanted to be alone. Leaving home was a rite of passage, as it should be for all young adults, and I was loving it. I was able to balance my classes along with a job and a serious girlfriend.

My major was performing arts. I still had a dream of becoming an actor. Just like when I made the move to the Lab School, college allowed me to see a brighter side of the world. I was surrounded by a diverse group of peers undertaking the same challenges as me: school, girls, friends, parties, and work.

I was no saint. I did my fair share of partying, but I always knew my limits. I rarely let things get out of my control. I knew I had to get my shit done, and I wasn't about to let partying too hard get in the way. I did just enough to enjoy myself and experience the freedom of not being under my father's wing.

During these years, my mother's murder was not in the forefront of my mind. I was busy trying to become something. I was focused on myself; my classes, my work, and making sure I was balancing everything. By this time, she had been dead a dozen years.

That is crazy to think about. A dozen years.

I would think of her often, especially on holidays and birthdays, and I still went with my father for the annual painting of the vault; but the weight of her absence grew more bearable as the years went by. That is not to say that I wasn't still operating in survival mode—I was. I was still living with the trauma, but it was no longer overtaking my life or consuming me. I wasn't checking in with my father as much as I used to, making sure he made it home from work and other functions. I wasn't paralyzed with fear by the frequent gunshots I heard in the neighborhood, or the alarms blaring from vandalized cars.

To be honest, I rarely thought of my father during these early years of living college, which is not unlike most early college students. We had our time together, and now it was time for us to be apart. He still wanted me to help him run his business, and I did so because that was what *he* wanted, not because I wanted to. I cut my teeth on the business, learning how to make deals and how *not* to make deals. I discovered many things about myself during this time, trying my best to make it work.

All those hours my father spent drilling me, forcing me to read and write, had built a work ethic in me that was now bearing fruit. I knew how to work hard, and I liked hard work. I loved throwing myself into something and feeling successful. Work felt natural and normal to me—comfortable. It still does. Work and me, we add up. I can throw myself completely into a project or a task and lose myself in it. I enjoy keeping my mind and my hands busy. I don't have an ounce of laziness in me. This is not me being prideful—it's just the truth. My father taught me the art of hustle, and to this day, I hate idle time. I prefer to be up and moving rather than relaxing.

I've learned that this, too, is a trauma response. It is hard for me to be still. In the stillness, the thoughts and feelings from the past sneak back in, and I begin to worry about what the future will look like after the trial. It is easy to get caught up and swept away by the torrent of emotions.

I don't allow it. I stay busy. I hustle. I work. But I know you can only outrun something for so long, and I feel the breath of the past on my neck.

THE TRIAL

The trial for my mother's murder is less than two months away and I find myself thinking about it—consumed by it—far too often. It is surreal to imagine that my father's fate will be decided by twelve complete strangers.

This is our legal system. It is due process. But when it's your own father it feels so wrong.

It feels harsh, and unfair.

I won't be allowed to attend the trial because I am a witness for the defense—as I should be. The thought of not knowing what is happening from day to day is paralyzing. Sometimes I have nightmares about what it will be like, and I see myself as that wide-eyed six-year-old boy, standing up and yelling out loud for the whole courtroom to hear: "That's my father! Leave him alone! You've all got this so terribly wrong! He didn't do anything wrong!"

I see myself screaming, sobbing, beating my little fists against the courtroom tables and slamming water glasses and files against the walls and floor, shaking everyone by the shoulders and screaming "You've got this all wrong. It's not supposed to be this way . . . somebody help him . . . somebody help me . . ." No one moves. They are completely frozen; motionless. No one even looks at me.

This is a terrible nightmare. I wake, my heart pounding and fists clenched, fingernails digging into my palms. My face is burning red and swollen, and my head pounds from decades of tears that fall like a downpour. I am drenched in salty sweat and tears as I realize no one is moving or listening because the yelling, pounding, screaming, smashing, and sobbing is inaudible to everyone but me. This battle only exists within my own mind and body, raging deep within, and I am the only one who can hear my cries for help.

It has always been this way. Lonely. Buried. Alone. A frantic son trying to keep it together, trying to mourn the loss of his mother *and* protect his father from life in prison. Somehow, I am left desperately alone and carrying the weight, and it is heavier than I am willing to admit. Admitting this seems like an invitation for it to finally overtake and consume me completely. There is no one to protect my father—no one. There sure as hell is no one to protect me. I am no longer that six-year-old boy, but the rage, intensity, anguish, and complexity of feelings remain frozen in time, sitting just below the surface, as if they have been awaiting my return.

And here I am.

The painful truth is that I cannot protect my father. My testimony may not protect him. I have no idea what the prosecution will ask of me or how they will attempt to spin my stories and maneuver my words to paint my father as someone who could take his wife's life.

Plus, I am tired of keeping it together.

I am weary of merely surviving. I am exhausted. When does *my* life begin?

The screams, fist pounding, and sobbing needs to exist out-side of my body, reverberating, projecting far and wide and deep for all to see and hear. Other people need to see and hear my pain and suffering and witness my anguish and despair. I need to release it into the wild, allowing the earth to open and absorb all that I have held onto for far too long.

How the hell did I get here?

Why the hell did *I* get dealt this hand?

As if a murdered mother is not enough for one person to han-dle in one lifetime, now I am forced to consider the possibility of losing my father, too? Why? How am I supposed to endure another loss? Will this be the one that finally takes me out, cuts me off at the knees and leaves me incapacitated? Will the weight finally crush me? There is so much in the balance, and yet every-thing is completely out of my control. There is not a damn thing I can do about any of it. That kind of lack of control is enough to drive a person crazy. I feel like I have never been in control of my life, and that's a super fucked up feeling.

So, as the days tick on and the trial date nears, I do what I have always done—I survive.

EXITS

I suppose living my life in survival mode and navigating the world with a great deal of fear that the other shoe will drop at any minute has had some benefits.

I know that sounds crazy.

I wouldn't choose it if I *had* a choice, but I didn't. So, I have learned to make it work. I handle it because that's what I do. There are many things about me that I wish everyone knew, and, since this is *my* book—*my* memoir—please indulge me as I share some of those things with you.

1. I feel deeply.

While this may seem like a weakness—especially in Black male culture—I have found it to be one of the things I like most about myself. If you are in my life, I care deeply about you, your family, and the things that you are passionate about. I never have been and never will be a fair-weather friend. If we are friends, I've got your back, and I always will. I am a consistent presence in the lives of those I care about. This makes me a great friend, a good husband, and hopefully an amazing father. Caring deeply can be hard. I internalize a lot of hurt and disappointment. I overanalyze and overthink things.

2. I am sensitive.

I feel everything. If you are struggling, I struggle with you. I will carry your burdens and lighten your load even if you don't ask me to; especially if you *don't* ask me to. I am like a dry sponge soaking up the emotions of the people around me. I can read a room within seconds. This heightened sensitivity or hypervigilance (also a trauma response) can at times be both a blessing and a curse. I absorb it all, the good and the bad, and it affects me both physically and emotionally, sometimes for days. It is crazy that I don't allow others to do the same for me. I cannot express in words how hard it is for me to ask for help. I have spent a lifetime learning how to handle things on my own. But you know . . . trauma.

3. I am reliable.

If I say I am going to do something, it is going to get done. Not just sort of done—all the way done and done well. I don't take shortcuts or half-ass things, and I always make good on my word. This has allowed me to move up the ranks at work and become highly successful in my career. It is hard not to see that this was instilled in me by my father. His high standards and expectations set my path into motion as a young boy. I may not always make the best grades, but you could count on me to try my best and keep trying. I was always reaching for the unattainable expectations my father set for me. Even when I would fall squarely on my face, I would get up and try again. My father didn't have much patience for giving up, and therefore, neither do I.

4. I am trustworthy.

You can count on me 110% of the time. I do not fail people. I always come through, even if I must sacrifice my own time, energy, and resources. I am the guy you want with you if the place goes up in flames. I know where the exits are, because . . . trauma. I will not hesitate to throw your ass over my shoulder and get you out of that burning building, and once I've got you out, I will run back in and get as many people as possible over my shoulder and out of that burning building. The same goes for relationships or circumstances that have gone up in flames or have succumbed to the scorching heat. I will always stand by your side and help you figure things out until you turn to me and say, "Get me the hell out of here, Reggie." You can count on my shoulder to carry you and my shoulder to lean on. The fires may be raging around us, but I will never allow you to burn. I like this part of myself, but I also recognize that it puts a lot of pressure on me. And performance-based pressure is how I got here, after all.

5. I am the guy you want around when the shit hits the fan, and all hell breaks loose.

I can handle some shit like it's just an ordinary Tuesday, because . . . trauma. It is what it is. I am who I am at this moment, but that's not to say I'm not working on it. I am working on allowing others to keep *me* safe. I am working on allowing others to rescue *me*. I am working on being the one who gets saved. This may be a life-long journey of unlearning and relearning; letting go of the feeling that I must always be in control and trusting that I can rely on others to keep *me* from the flames. But, for now, what you see is what you get. I don't have the time or energy to be fake. I am upfront and straight forward. I recognize that there are parts of myself that I hide because of the trauma, but I am not doing it intentionally. I am practicing being more open, speaking my truth, and letting it live outside of my own heart and mind. I don't have the time, energy, or patience for pretenses, nor do I have the time, energy, or patience for others who do. Life is too damn short for all that.

With me, you know exactly what you're dealing with.

RUMORS

I have only heard rumors of what happened to my mother the night she was murdered. You know how stories go; facts and gossip stretched and misconstrued over decades as people recall and relay details as they have heard them. It is like a kindergarten game of telephone. By the time the details reached me they were a shadow of what they had been in the beginning. I have lived among these rumors my entire life.

"Did you hear . . . ?"

"Did you hear that murdered woman was having an affair with . . . ?"

"Why in the world was she out all alone?"

"I heard she may be pregnant, and *not* by her husband!"

"Did you hear . . . ?"

Almost nothing was based on the facts, only rumors. People like to talk, but they *love* to gossip. It must have been hard on the community to witness a cold case unfold, the possibility of a murderer walking free among them. People don't like unresolved things; they like answers. Resolution. In most cases, they begin to construct their own ideas of what may have taken place in the absence of cold hard facts. They take bits and pieces of what they have heard—most of which may not even be true—and create a story. They often have little regard for the effects that their imaginings may have when they reach the ears of surviving family, especially a young son.

Rumors became another part of my life.

There were all manner of rumors surrounding my father as well. When someone is murdered, the spouse is almost immediately a person of interest. So it was with my father. The police questioned him and questioned other people about him; however, no charges were ever brought forward against my father. He was cleared, but that didn't stop the rumor mill from churning.

It wasn't overt, but just enough to get under a person's skin. People staring and talking in hushed tones in the corner of a restaurant, whispered theories of what may have happened, and false narratives constructed to ease their own minds. While I do believe someone—or possibly multiple people—know exactly what took place that night, gossipy neighbors didn't know anything.

As I got older and social media—namely Facebook— became a thing, the rumors intensified. Any time there was something in the paper about the murder, people had all sorts of things to say on Facebook. They would sit behind their computer screens in their false anonymity and type out some of the ugliest things you can imagine.

I have always wanted to know the truth, and to know exactly what occurred that night. I hold on to the supposition that the imaginations and wonderings of our minds are most often far worse than reality.

WOUNDS

Wounds heal in layers—the physical and the emotional. This magic of the human body resonates deeply with me as I examine my childhood wounds. There is the most obvious and deepest wound, the murder of my mother. The wound caused by her being ripped away from my life as I knew it and her palpable absence. The fact that she is never coming home. There one day, gone the next.

This kind of loss and trauma does something to a kid, even if I could not feel it or articulate it then. It did something to me that can never be fully repaired. My mother's brutal murder and the impact of her absence during my childhood, adolescence, and teen years made a deep indelible mark that will stay with me until my final breath.

My wound is deep, wide, and jagged. My wound doesn't have perfect edges or clear-cut lines. It is more like a tear than a clean cut, the skin ripped and violently gashed. It is the worst kind of wound you can imagine. As a boy, it was a gaping jagged-edged hole more painful than I can even begin to describe. If I had to pinpoint its location it would be right over my beating heart, a constant searing pain across my entire chest. As a six-year-old boy, the pain would rear its ugly head whenever I began to forget, reminding me of its never-ending presence. I would be going about my day and suddenly remember that my mother is dead, and I will never see her again.

In these moments my chest would begin to feel heavy, the wound becoming a physical ache while the sting of it sucked the breath right out of my tiny little lungs. For the most part, this happened in private. Wounds don't like to be exposed, preferring to remain hidden deep in the dark where only the bearer feels their unwavering presence. As a young boy, I was ruled by my wound. I couldn't escape it because I had not yet learned the coping skills needed to manage the pain. This meant that I felt everything.

Everything.

I was an exposed nerve ending just waiting to be triggered. Even though I didn't possess the words to adequately express how this felt, nor did I have the life experience needed to fully understand the power the wound had over me, I felt every emotion as though I was boy and grown man all at once.

Children shouldn't have to feel pain that deeply.

Childhood was hard not simply because my mother was gone, and my father was a hard man to live with. I had a deep wound that was very real to me, but invisible to everyone else. Not a day went by that it didn't try its hardest to bring me to my knees; and many days, it did just that.

The pressure of my father's expectations combined with my struggles in school left me feeling alone and misunderstood. I never felt like I was enough. I desperately needed a mother to help me navigate my way in the world. My constant confusion over the circumstances of her death and learning to live with the constant speculation and rumors were like pouring salt on the wound in my chest.

It is a miracle I made it through those early years. If I had to do it all over again, I'm not sure I would fare as well. As I grew older, the wound began to bind itself up, the passage of time creating layers of new skin over the hole in my chest. In my middle years, I became better able to manage the pain. I did what most teenagers do: Instead of feeling, I went numb. I ignored the wound. I pretended it was not there at all. For the most part, this strategy worked well for me. I was enjoying life as a young man, so self-focused that the wound left me alone. It was like an agreement between me and the pain: You leave me alone, and I'll leave you alone.

You and I both know that this is a fool's bargain. The wound was and still is right where it always was. Ignoring it or numbing out does nothing to heal our deepest hurts. It is just like pressing pause; the pain will be there waiting for you when all the distractions no longer do the trick. Wounds cannot be ignored forever; eventually, they demand our attention.

I noticed that familiar ache returning in the early years of my marriage and fatherhood.

I wanted my mother.

I needed my mother.

I *deserved* my mother.

I longed for her, and the ripped edges of my wound would begin to smart and ache again. I would think of her, my emotions bubbling up and causing tears to flow.

I miss my mother. I miss my mother. I miss my mother.

Though I don't have enough memories of her to know exactly what I miss about her, I still feel a deep empty place in my life where her presence would have and should have been. The wound swells and contracts in time with the beating of my heart. It is an old scar and reminds me of all that has been lost; how deeply I have been hurt, and the painful truth of all that was taken from me. My wound and scars are a part of me, and I am fiercely protective of them. I hate to admit that they inform how I live, but that is the truth of it. The worst part is, there is no golden ticket to ensure that because I have already experienced such deep pain and loss I won't be hurt again, just as deeply as I was as a young boy.

I bob and weave through life, doing my best to avoid any possibility of being hurt again. I create safety nets around myself, and by proxy, my small family. If I can control my life and everything in it, I am safe. This makes life tricky. The relentless pursuit of safety and control is exhausting. Relationships are hard and people can be fickle, easily disappointing us or falling short of our expectations. They are only human after all.

Allowing another person into my life means I may get hurt. They may leave, or decide I am too wounded. They may go out one night and never come home. They may die. I stay guarded, even with those that I dearly love. If I am being brutally honest, I am most guarded with those that I love the most. This is the unfair reality of living with someone who has survived trauma. My wife is aware of my wounds, but I know that I can be hard to live with.

My son is not yet old enough to be aware of it, but someday he will be, and I fear that it will somehow rob our relationship of all the special experiences and bonds a father and son deserve. I fear this because I have lived this exact dynamic with my father. When I think about this it is hard not to get angry. I want to beat my chest with my fists right where the wound lies and tell it to go the fuck away.

It has stolen so much already. So much time. So many experiences. So much love. No more. You can't have any more of my life. The wound tells me that I must deal with it before it will loosen its grip on me. I must stare into the deep chasm of hurt, sadness, and grief. I must acknowledge the pain caused by its jagged edges. This is the work. This is the messy middle of healing.

I am standing before my reflection in the mirror with tear-filled eyes and clenched fists, staring straight at the wound. I bring my hand to my chest and outline the place where I feel the hurt. My heart races. It is much larger than I thought. Once covering the tiny chest of a six-year-old boy it now encompasses my entire adult chest. It is ugly, and it doesn't like to be exposed to so much light. It aches. I keep staring, slowly tracing the ragged edges.

It hesitantly agrees, feeling just as afraid as me. It has grown comfortable there, like a crucial part of my being. If I ask it to leave, maybe I won't survive . . . I take a deep breath, my shoulders rising and falling. I feel a shift, a release. There is a glimmer of hope. For the first time in my life, I can almost imagine an existence without the wound. I can no longer live my life in a place of brokenness. I *must* heal. It is time. I am ready to begin.

I speak the words slowly, broken, cracking with emotion: "Let's do this."

VISITING THE POST

I have not been home in years, so last month I made a trip home to visit my father. My wife and I packed up the car and made the long journey across Texas to the tiny house on Apple Street. You know that feeling you get when you visit a place from your past, where everything that once seemed so big and important now feels so very small and insignificant? The trees, once large and healthy, are now mere shadows of their former selves. An overwhelming feeling of disappointment mixed with nostalgia hit me as we slowly pulled into the narrow gravel driveway of my childhood home.

The house looked so small, as if it had been shrunk into a miniature version of itself. It seemed almost unimaginable that my father and I could have lived here. How did our lives and all that we were carrying not bust the seams and crack open the roof? How did this tiny house that I had come to call The Post contain us?

The house had seen better days. My father had done his best to keep it up, but it was definitely showing the wear and tear of age. The outside seemed so very gray. A layer of dust and grime covered every inch of the exterior, the color having been sucked out of its boards and bricks years ago. The house looked lifeless. The sadness of that fact sank in, and my chest felt the all too familiar ache of grief.

My wife, son, and I sat in the car for a long time before I was ready to go inside. My mind flooded with thoughts and memories—some good, and some bad. A lot had happened within those walls, and I suddenly felt ill-equipped to handle the rush of the past. My wife reached for my hand. I hadn't realized that I was still clutching the steering wheel long after putting the car in park.

Her gentle touch startled me. I was deep in my memories, gray specters from my past flashing across my mind like reels in an old cinema. I was seeing, feeling, and hearing them in waves, unable to pause or turn them off altogether. I consciously told my hand to relax into hers. We sat that way, hand in hand, for what seemed like an eternity. The baby was asleep, the car warm and quiet. I wasn't ready to go inside. I wanted to stay here. I wanted to stay safe. At last, I turned to my wife, and we locked eyes. I saw compassion there. She knew that my mind was racing and that this was not going to be an easy visit.

"You ready?" she asked tentatively.

"No," I said quietly. I wasn't ready now and was unsure whether I ever would be.

This trip would be an emotionally charged roller coaster. The fact of the matter was that this very well could be the last time I see my father as a free man; the last time I set foot inside my childhood home. The next trip to The Post could look very different. I was keenly aware of the purpose and magnitude of this trip. We were here to see my father. If he is convicted, we may never get to see him again without steel bars between us. The reality of this was like a sucker punch straight to the gut. It knocks the wind out of me, and I struggle to take a deep breath. I squeeze my wife's hand.

A light Louisiana afternoon rain began to fall, and I knew that it was now or never. We gathered our things, woke the baby, and quickly shuffled to the front door, the familiar sound of gravel crunching beneath my feet. I was glad to have the rain as my motivation to get through the door, although I could have lingered there on the porch with my thoughts just as easily as I had inside the car.

The front door opened, and my internal swirling slowed to a stop as we hugged my father and watched him meet his grandson for the very first time. I am completely and utterly surprised by the pure joy in this moment. For just a little while, joy has taken the place of my inner turmoil, and I allow myself to simply watch them get to know one another. Lathan's eyes are wide, taking it in as he and my father connect instantly. He is my father in miniature. I sit back and soak in as much as I can, fighting to stay fully present in the moment. It would be so easy to fall back into the painful memories of the past or fixate on the unknown anxieties of the future.

Sometimes when this battle is raging within me, fighting for my presence, it helps to anchor my body and in so doing, my mind. I leaned against the hallway door frame to stabilize myself, to stay in the moment and slow the swirling within. My childhood bedroom is just footsteps away. I will not enter that room on this trip; I don't know that I will ever enter it again.

Lathan and my father continue to enjoy one another with abandon, laughing, tickling, and playing with toys on the floor.

My father is mesmerized, as is Lathan. I stand still, anchored, watching, fighting to *stay*. It is all at once the most beautiful and the most heartbreaking moment of my life. My son. My father. Two of the most important figures in my life meeting for the first—and perhaps the last—time.

Joy can be so fleeting at times. When you really allow yourself to sink down in it and lose yourself in the magic of a given moment, something happens. It is like flipping a switch in your mind, and you can go from joy and peace to fear and dread in a millisecond.

If you have ever stood over your sleeping child and felt full of love, joy, and hope, only to feel terrified the next second, you know what I am talking about. You are terrified that this precious child of yours who brings you so much love and joy could be ripped away at any moment. You recognize the fragility of life and that no one is promised forever; there are no guarantees. Children get hurt. Children die. My world could fall apart in an instant.

This is how the trip home felt for me. I vacillated between joy and fear the entire time. One moment I was enjoying a conversation with my father, and in the next breath, without warning, I would catch myself wondering if this would be the last normal conversation we would ever have. Would this be the last meal we shared? My mind flooded with memories of hundreds, if not thousands of meals we had shared at our tiny kitchen table. Would this be the last time my father would hold his only grandson? The last time he would touch his tiny face, kiss his chubby cheeks, and tickle his round baby belly?

Some of the flashbacks I had while visiting The Post included my mother. They weren't actual memories, but everyday situations I have contrived in my mind in which she is very much present. I allow myself to see time spent as a family around the dinner table, my mother standing in the kitchen cooking or helping me with my homework. I imagine her in the car with us, curly hair blowing in the warm late summer breeze as she turns around to offer a smile before sticking her beautiful brown hand out the window to bob in the wind without a care in the world.

It is easy to imagine her in this house somehow. Maybe it is because I am a parent now and am all too familiar with the roles we play in the lives of our children, especially when they are young and need us the most. I have witnessed my wife in the role of mother to our son. I know a bit about what this looks like in action. I assume my mother was no different, doting and loving, always putting my needs before her own.

I immerse myself in a good bit of wishful thinking as well; wishing my mother were there with me now, wishing things were different. Wishing I could go back and change everything, and that this whole trip wasn't overshadowed by the fact that it *could* be the last. I experience many moments when I feel led to latch on to my father like a young boy would. I imagine wrapping my arms around his neck, holding on as tight as I could, and wishing I could press pause and stay this way forever.

It is as if we are covered by a dark cloud, a constant reminder that this could all be ripped away in a matter of months. There's just never enough time when you start to consider the possibilities. There are never the right words to convey all that you are feeling or want to share, never enough hugs or pats on the back. There are never enough *thank you's* and *I'm sorry's*. Never enough *it's okay,* or *I understand*.

There is never enough *time*.

PART THREE

THE WAITING

THE AUTOPSY REPORT

I was given fair warning that once I saw the contents of the autopsy report there would be things—lots of things—that I could never unhear or unsee. Even with this stern warning, I still wanted to see and read everything for myself. I had lived on rumors and gossip most of my life, and I wanted to see what happened to my mother that night with my own eyes.

The email arrived with the simple subject line: *Autopsy*.

I clicked open the email without hesitation. In the text there was yet another warning about the contents of the report. I read over it quickly, my fingers immediately clicking to open the large file attached. Without reading, I hit *print*. I wanted to feel the pages in my hands; to hold the truth once and for all. It was time for me to know—to *see*—the truth no matter how intense or hard it would be to stomach. As the printer shot out page after page of reports and photographs, I convinced myself that I was prepared for whatever I would see or read about the murder of my mother. What I didn't consider was how I would *feel* after taking in all of this information.

At first, I wasn't rattled. I read each page slowly, pouring over each detail and sometimes retracing my steps, rereading whole sections, or pausing to look up medical or forensic terms that I didn't understand. I underlined key details, circling things that brought up questions. I made copious notes in the margins of every page.

In the beginning, I read with the eye of an amateur detective. During the first few hours I spent pouring over the report I searched for clues, trying to connect the dots while doing my best to make sense of what I was reading. There was so much information and much of it had never made its way into the whispered conversations and rumors that I had lived with up to this point.

This was the *truth*.

One thing was crystal clear to me: My mother's murder was more violent and brutal than I had ever imagined. I am sure you've heard the saying "It's never worse than what you imagine." Not in this case. In this case, my imagination hadn't even begun to scratch the surface. I had no idea just how barbaric and vicious the attack on her body was, and the horrific brutality that ended her life. I read the descriptions and stared into the photos of my mother's naked body. Close-up images showed the wounds covering her chest and neck. I could see just how forceful and unrelenting her murderer had been.

The realization that another person or persons could inflict this magnitude of violence against another human being—especially my mother—was too much to bear.

NECROPSY (AUTOPSY) PROTOCOL

NAME: REED, SELONIA O.	**NECROPSY NO.** —
HOSPITAL NUMBER —	**AGE** 26 **RACE** B **SEX** F
DATE & TIME ADMITTED — **DOB:** 12-13-60	**WARD** — **SERVICE** —
DATE & TIME OF DEATH 8-23-87	**DATE & TIME AUTOPSIED** 8-24-87; 9:00
(REDACTED) **Acting Coroner**	**PROSECUTOR** (REDACTED)
CORONER'S CASE TANGIPAHOA PARISH	

FINAL DIAGNOSIS

1. Multiple stab wounds to the thorax and the right neck with/including:
   a. Perforation of the right lung and heart (right atrium.)
   b. Diffuse subcutaneous hemorrhage of the soft tissues of the right neck.
   c. Right hemothorax, mediastinal hemorrhage and hemopericardium.
2. Multiple abrasions of the neck left shoulder and back, both earlobes.
3. Focal subarachnoid hemorrhage left partial lobe.
4. Bilateral hematoma on temporalis muscle.

CAUSE OF DEATH:
Internal hemorrhage due to stab wounds to the chest.

MANNER OF DEATH:
Homicide

AUTOPSY PERMISSION:
Autopsy authorized by Acting Coroner of Tangipahoa Parish,(Redacted)

ATTENDING AUTOPSY:
(All Names Redacted)

CIRCUMSTANCES OF DEATH:
This is a body of a young Black female found dead in her car with an umbrella inserted in her vagina. She was found dead at 9:30 AM, 8-23-87, in a parking lot off Highway 190, Hammond, LA.

EXTERNAL EXAMINATION:
The body is first observed lying supine on a stretcher at (location removed) hospital morgue. The body is completely flaccid and shows evidence of early decomposition. General inspection reveals copious amounts of blood dried on the face, mixed with pink foam and mucoid material protruding from both nostrils. The tip of the tongue is trapped between upper and lower incisors.

EVIDENCE OF INJURY:

1. A cluster of 7 stab wounds to the right anterior chest wall oriented transversely and diagonally. They measure .5 cm each with both extremes of the wounds appearing sharply angulated.

The skin of my mother's face had been peeled back during the autopsy. Her head rested on a block of wood, her scalp and hair hanging over the edge. The examination table was not a table at all, but a black metal grate. I assume this is so bodily fluids and blood would drain rather than accumulate during the examination. Her chest is splayed open to reveal bloated organs. Her intestines spill from her body, swollen and distended. She is bloody, bruised, bloated, torn, pulled apart, shredded, and gashed. She has been mutilated.

This photo before me is of a woman that I can barely recognize.

My mother was first killed and then mutilated in order to discover how she lost her life. It seems cruel, and I struggle to make sense of it. How can the woman in this photo be my mother? What have they done to her? Her face. Her poor, beautiful face is stripped away, revealing mangled tissue and bone.

No one can prepare you for seeing an image like this. She looks like a lab experiment gone terribly wrong, something not even human. Her body is broken, pierced, and torn beyond my most vivid imaginings. I am finally seeing the truth. I will no longer be able to retreat to the comfort of rumors and gossip.

This is the truth, and the truth is fucking awful.

CRIME SCENE

The many photos and crime scene video confirm my assumption that my mother was killed somewhere other than inside her vehicle. Someone placed her naked body in the passenger seat of the car after the crime had been committed. I stared at the photos in front of me. She is lying on her side, legs stretched out into the passenger wheel well, the umbrella visible between her legs. Her head is angled towards the back seat of the car.

Someone took great effort to place her this way—*exactly* this way.

There are little to no signs of blood inside the car, indicating that she must have been murdered elsewhere, her body drained of every ounce of blood before being placed inside the car. There are no signs of a struggle taking place inside the vehicle. Everything is in its place, orderly, and clean.

The images are horrific and surreal. How could this be my mother? How could someone do this to my mother? Besides the sick and twisted use of the umbrella, my mother's body had been covered in some sort of thick white liquid. It appears to have been smeared on her body after she was placed in the car.

My eyes slowly survey each detail of the photo—until I get to her face.

I have to stop.

I have to look away.

The lawyer was right. I could not and would not ever be able to unsee the images before me. They will haunt me for the rest of my life, scrolling like reels beside brutal descriptions of how she was taken from me, all playing on repeat in my mind forever.

Another layer of grief sets in. I return to the files the next day. I am a glutton for punishment, I suppose. So many years of not knowing has baited my curiosity. The second day is immensely more difficult. This time I looked at the information from a son's perspective. My heart is broken, shattered into a million pieces, and then crushed by the weight of this new level of grief. I can't look away.

The pain is already so raw and my need to know so strong that I look at every single document again. This time, I notice details that hadn't stood out to me during the first pass. Certain pieces of evidence and phrases describing the murder and the scene land on me differently than the day before. It is not because I was looking at the information with a fresh set of eyes. Quite the contrary. I am exhausted, worn out, and completely drained. I feel as though I have run a marathon, stayed up all night drinking, and then been run over by an 18-wheeler on a gravel road. My emotions are heightened, my body is rigid and tight. I'm just looking for a reason to snap at anyone or anything.

I feel raw, the images pouring over me like salt in a freshly cut wound.

I look away. The images are too hard to look at. *This is too much.*

For the first time in a very long time, I cry. I am unable to contain the ocean of grief within me any longer. Deep guttural sobs overtake me, hot tears pouring out of my tired eyes and down my face, forming small puddles on the photos of my mother. I don't wipe them away.

I sit there, hunched over my desk, for what feels like forever. I vacillate between silent tears and violent sobs, shoulders rising and falling, my chest aching with tension and heartbreak. Until this day I don't think I have ever really allowed myself to feel the magnitude of my grief, or release the sadness I had been holding onto, and there was an abundance of tears to be shed.

I have chills as I write these words. Once you strip everything else away—the anger, pain, loss, and trauma—all that is left is an endless well of sadness. It takes hold and completely consumes me.

I weep for my mother.

I weep for *all* the layers of her that I will never know, and the layers of me she never got to know.

I weep for the fear and torture she must have felt as her life was being brutally taken.

I weep for my father; grieving widower, single father, and now suspect in my mother's murder.

At last, I fall into a restless sleep. I had never dreamt of my mother until this night. I have always hoped to and wanted to see her in my dreams. There have been times when I felt the essence of her in my dreams, but never before have I seen her fully embodied there. This is the first time that she took on her full form.

The dream started as chaos, pieces of my life mixing and swirling together in a mad cacophony. Nothing made sense, but I could feel the turmoil. Then, there she was. She came in flashes and bursts, like lightning. I see her face, young and beautiful, the same face that I had seen in photos or brought forth from my memory. She is happy, with a soft easy smile on her lips. Her face is relaxed and content.

I will her to look at me.

"Look at me! I'm right here, please look at me!" My voice is a frenzied mixture of my six-year-old and 39-year-old selves.

"Just look at me, Mommy! Look at me—please!"

She turns toward me slowly. Her face changes at this moment. It is no longer the beautiful fully alive face that I long to see, but has become the sunken grey face of death, the face from the autopsy photo.

"No!" I scream. "No! Go back, go back, go back . . ."

She can't hear my screams, and she does not go back. I reach out toward her face, my hand shaking. I convince myself that my touch will bring her back to life. As my hand touches her cheek, I wake up. I lie in bed shaking, my body drenched in a cold sweat.

For several moments I am terrified. It takes me a while to get my bearings, eyes scanning the room and my surroundings. My wife is asleep beside me. I steady myself and lean back against the headboard, managing one long, labored breath.

I exhale slowly and begin to cry.

WHEN THE FIRE IS BLAZING

*"Americans are really good at acute compassion, but
pretty bad at chronic empathy . . . We don't like being care
workers, we want to be heroes. The world does not need more
heroes. We need more care."*

—SIGRID ELLIS

When tragedy strikes, sirens blaring and fires blazing, people respond in full force. In the midst of tragedy, you are surrounded by people. Everyone shows up. Everyone wants to warm themselves by the fireside of your misfortune. They offer food, condolences, and copious amounts of thoughts and prayers. After the fire begins to burn out, people start to fall away. The lights are not as bright. They can no longer warm themselves by your flames, so they get cold, and simply go away.

A person's capacity for compassion is often measured and short-lived. Ellis's observation of this human phenomenon is spot on. People want to be the heroes of your story, not the caring and committed sidekicks. This has been my life. My entire life. When I sit alone in the quiet, the feeling that causes me the most heartbreak is the fear that nobody really gives a shit.

Not about my mom.

Not about me.

Not about my dad.

Not about my family.

Not about the trial.

People.

Don't.

Give.

A.

Shit.

I haven't heard from anyone in my family, not on my mother's or father's side. No calls, texts, cards, or letters. Nothing. Complete silence. They avoid me. How hard could it be to just check in? What is *wrong* with people? Are they really that self-absorbed, unable to see beyond their own lives? I'm not asking them to drop everything and rush to my side. I simply want some sort of recognition that what I have been through and am now going through matters.

That *I* matter.

I don't expect much. *Hey, I am so sorry this is happening to you, Reggie*, would be great. Or *it's so unfair that you have to go through all this, Reggie*, would be nice. Validation that this situation is awful and that I am caught in the swirling middle of it would certainly ease some of the burden. In the absence of validation, I allow myself to go numb. I must have been crazy to expect anything from anyone.

I don't feel seen or heard. I don't feel understood. No one except Quentin and my wife even try to understand me. So, here I sit, with only the support of my wife, godfather, and one solid childhood friend, Quentin.

This is a lonely place to be.

The subject line of the email reads "CRIME SCENE VIDEO." I had completely forgotten about my request until now. I stare at the computer screen with a mixture of terror and curiosity. My heart races as I click open the message. There is a warning:

Reggie,
This video is graphic and will be disturbing. Watch with
discretion.

A link highlighted in electric blue stares back at me. *I've already seen the autopsy photos, so how much more graphic could it be?* I think. To hell with it. I click the link, waiting impatiently for the video to download. I hit play. A grainy video opens with a time stamp in the top right corner:

11:19 a.m.
8.23.87

The video begins to play, wavy lines and static bouncing across my screen as the picture comes into focus. I hear the muffled sound of men's voices and the crunch of gravel under feet. The person holding the video recorder approaches my mother's car from behind. Three men are gathered at the front of the car talking—I can't make out what is being said—and gesturing toward the vehicle. A fourth man is opening the driver's side door, looking inside. It strikes me that there is no urgency in their demeanor, or panic in their voices. I remind myself that they've been in this position before, standing next to the dead body of a woman in a car.

There are no other cars in the parking lot. Her car is parked beside a building, but I can't make out the type, or where it is. It looks like an old storage unit or building that is no longer in use. The killer did not attempt to hide the car, that much is clear. The summer foliage in front of the car is bright green, over-grown with grass and weeds. It is the end of August in Louisiana and according to the time stamp, it's coming up on noon. Even though the sky is slightly overcast, I can feel the desperate heat. I think of painting the vault and unconsciously wipe my forehead on my sleeve. The camera pans around my mother's small blue car and zooms in on the passenger side window.

There she is. The crunch of gravel stops as the camera takes time to capture the entire scene. *Perhaps I should have taken the advice of the sender, "Watch with discretion,"* I think to myself. Too late now.

I see her.

My mother is completely naked, her body lying in the passenger seat, her back to the window. Her upper body has fallen and lies between the driver and passenger seats. I cannot see her face. I want to see her face. I can hear birds chirping in the background, and the gentle rustle of wind. That can't be right. How does the world go on after something like this? Why is the sun in the sky? Why is the wind blowing? I see no reason for the birds to sing today. I see no reason for the world to keep spinning.

I hit pause. I need a minute.

My eyes are glued to the screen, and I have forgotten to breathe. I force a short, shaky breath and lean my head back for a moment. I continue. The camera zooms in on her body, and I see the umbrella. I have read about the umbrella many times, but seeing it is something I am not prepared for. There is no delicate way to describe what I am seeing.

The handle end of the umbrella has been forced inside my mother's vagina.

What sick animal would do such a thing? I fight the urge to be sick. Her body is covered in a pasty white substance. It is all over her backside and torso. I still can't see her face. The camera pans to the front of the car. I can see that my mother's upper body has either fallen or been placed this way, wedged between the front seats. Her right arm lays at her side and her hand is in the driver's seat, fingers curled into a loose fist.

The voices become more distinguishable as the camera gets closer to the men in front of the car. They are discussing what they think may have happened, with no urgency or panic in their slow southern drawls. I am shocked by how calm they sound. "That's my mother in there!" I want to scream at them. The man with the camera walks around to the driver's side. The door is still open. A man gathers samples from the inside of the car, my mother's lifeless body just inches from his face. I see now that her entire stomach is covered in the white substance. It seems to have been placed there intentionally. *What sort of sick animal does such a thing*, I wonder again.

The video is 53.50 minutes long. I am only 1.07 minutes in. I force another shaky breath.

The camera zooms into the back seat of the car. Her left arm is stretched into the footwell. Her inner forearm is bruised and bloody. These are the only visible injuries to her body that I have seen thus far, other than the umbrella. I focus for a moment on the blood and wonder why, with a crime like this, there isn't more. The camera moves and zooms in on my mother's face.

I stop breathing.

It's bad.

It's so, so bad.

I look away. Tears sting my eyes, and I can no longer hold them back. Great sobs escape my throat as I try to catch my breath. Her face is unrecognizable. This monster has destroyed my mother's perfect, beautiful face. Her eyes are closed. Her nose, mouth, and chin are bashed in and mutilated. Her face is bruised, bloody, and so badly beaten that I can barely make out her features. Her nose is split open and collapsed. Whoever did this to her *intentionally* mutilated her face.

It again seems odd to me that I cannot see any significant injuries to her body other than the ones on her forearm, left hand, and face, and there is very little evidence of blood. There is no blood pooling around her body in the seat, or floorboards—no blood *anywhere*.

She was not killed here, I think. She was intentionally placed in the car after her body bled out. I imagine her killer—or killers—moving her body here, positioning her upright in the passenger seat, and then leaving, the weight of her body causing her to slump forward and toward the driver's seat as the decomposition process began. I can hear the officer at the driver's side gathering evidence, his tools wiping and scraping, as he gathers mud, dirt, and gravel. Suddenly, the voices become clear.

"So, when she didn't show up this morning at home when he woke up . . ." the officer's voice trails off.

They're talking about my father. They've already been in contact with him. *He already knows she is dead,* I think, as if I'm watching the scene unfold before me in real time. The video goes white for a moment, the static of 1980s VHS filling the screen before becoming clear again. Now, the camera is about 20 feet away and focused on the back of the car. One officer still gathering evidence on the driver's side.

I pause. *The video was edited and spliced.* The conversation between the officers that included the details of my mother not showing up at home and my father calling the police may have been deleted from the original video. I hear the sounds of cars driving by. These aren't Sunday driving sounds. These cars are passing by at a good speed. That means that her car must be near a highway or a county road, somewhere with higher speed limits. The officers discuss taking measurements, of what, I cannot make out over the sounds of the passing cars. They have been called in on a Sunday morning and are all dressed in plain civilian clothes, some even wearing baseball caps. I count three, maybe four officers. They are now all focused on the driver's side of the vehicle. No one has opened the passenger side door where my mother lies, lifeless.

The officers begin calling out all sorts of measurements. They are measuring the distance from the curb to the car, but they are doing so by measuring the building beside the vehicle.

"40 feet 4 inches," one of them says.

"51.6 . . . "

It is clear from the road noise and the measurements that the car was near the curb, which means that whoever did this did not try very hard to hide her, or the car. In fact, it's almost as if they wanted her to be found. Another man joins the officer who has been gathering samples. He is finished on the driver's side and the new officer moves to the passenger side of the car with what looks like a medical bag in hand.

"I've got some gauze, too."

The new officer opens the passenger door. No samples are taken from the passenger side door handle. No one is wearing gloves either, another detail that strikes me as odd. The new officer is squatted down wiping the inside of the door. The driver's side door remains open. Two officers continue to take measurements as the new officer wipes down the passenger side window.

The sun blazes overhead, and the officers take every opportunity to remove their ballcaps and wipe the sweat from their brows. They are still taking measurements, which at this moment seems inconsequential as there is the body of a dead woman—my mother—lying *inside* the car. What does it matter how far the front of her car is from the overgrown grass? How important is it to know the length and width of her car? These seem like details that could have been attended to *after* they focused on my mother. Can they even see her? I feel rage rising in me and hear myself shouting, "Somebody pay attention to my mother! Fuck the measurements, what about my mother?!"Ten minutes in and she is still lying there, invisible.

"I'm gonna measure right there where I did before. 35.6."

This dialogue goes on for what seems like forever. I hear the noise of a car arriving at the scene, and several new officers appear and gather on the driver's side. They bend over to look inside the car. One of them is a very tall man. I now know that this man was the Chief of Police.

"She bled a lot. A lot. She was beaten on really good. See all that blood on the side of her face? There's a fingerprint with blood over here on the hand. You take special care of that. There's a lot of blood somewhere . . . " His voice trails off.

They are discussing what needs to be done before they move her body, but I can't make out the details over the highway noise. Two uniformed officers walk into the scene. One is wiping the sweat from the back of his neck with a towel while the other has a white towel draped over his head. August in Louisiana. According to the clock in the video, it's almost noon. 18.45 minutes in.

I need a break.

────────

The remainder of the day passes, but I am unable to get the images of my mother's face out of my mind. Who would have hated her enough to mutilate her face? Who would do such a thing? Who could live with themselves after destroying her face? Who . . .? I know the world is full of evil but seeing that evil manifested in my own life has literally kicked the wind out of me. I struggle to breathe.

Breathe, Reggie. Breathe.

The cruelty and brutality are beyond comprehension. Breathe. . .Tears sting my eyes, pooling at the edge. I try not to cry as I play with my son, wanting desperately to keep this sorrow from him. It is no use, and the tears fall hot and slow, salty, and bitter. I begin to sob, my body heaving and shaking as my grief refuses to be contained any longer.

Breathe, Reggie. Breathe.

I can't sleep. I lie awake, replaying the scenes over and over again in my mind. One image lingers longer than the rest—her face. Her poor, beautiful face. My mother. What she must have gone through is unimaginable. Rather than lying awake all night, I decide to finish the video. *Be done with it*, I reason with myself. I make my way to the office, pull up the video, and watch it from the beginning once again.

I hit play and slide the timer back, hit play again, and slide the timer back again. I listen and watch more closely each time I replay it. I am still struck by the birds, the sound of the wind, the rushing sound of cars in the background, and especially the pace at which the officers move, without urgency. Why all the random measurements when a dead woman is lying in the car? Who would care how long and wide her car was? This is not what people would remember. These are not the images that would make their way into the newspapers then, or the internet and social media now. People would only care about the brutal way in which she was killed. They would only want to hear the salacious details about how someone sexually assaulted her with an umbrella and then covered her body in a thick white substance.

An hour or so has passed before I reached the 18.45 mark, the place where I left off earlier in the day. It occurs to me now that 18 minutes is not that long. The intensity of the circumstances has made time slow down, drawing out the minutes and seconds as if the clock is moving backward. I think this is a common emotion for people in the midst of trauma. Time creeps by. Everything becomes impossibly heavy, and nothing moves at a normal pace. It feels like wading waist-deep through thick mud. I hit play again.

"You take special care of those hands, now. And when you're done cover them with bags and tie it off with a rubber band." The chief repeats his initial instructions, adding the bits about bags and rubber bands.

That statement hits me like a gut punch.

There are now seven men gathered around the driver's side of the car. One is leaning in, his arm draped casually atop the car like it's an ordinary day and he's engaged in a leisurely conversation. The voices become muffled by what sounds like a plane passing overhead. An officer appears with a brown paper bag. He leans into the driver's side door, angling himself into the backseat. I can only assume that he is following instructions, placing that bag over my mother's blood-stained hand.

I feel gutted as I watch.

I can't wrap my head around or fully appreciate the level of care they are taking to preserve evidence. I am not watching a crime show on television. This is personal. That is *my mother's* bloody hand being bagged. That is the hand that held my hand, checked me for fever when I was sick, and lifted my chin when I was sad. My soul knows this, not because I have specific memories of her doing it but because that's what mothers do for their young sons. *I know this.* Tears run down my cheeks, my chin…I can't believe I still have tears left to shed. *Breathe, Reggie. Breathe.*

The timestamp now reads 11:57 a.m. The sun beats down with merciless fury. The officers continuously wipe sweat from their foreheads. The camera pans to the inside of the vehicle, focusing on the passenger side where my mother's body lies. You can see one leg is bare all the way down to her missing shoe. Her jeans are pulled down around her calf on the other leg, one white tennis shoe still on her foot. From this angle, the umbrella can clearly be seen, shoved between her legs and into her vagina. Her skin has begun to darken in certain areas, an indication that her body has begun to decompose. Rigor is setting in. She has been here for well over eight hours.

It is 12:01 p.m. At last, an officer wheels in a gurney.

"You know this is going to be a challenge," the officer says. I notice that he is wearing gloves. He reaches in to move my mother's body but can't. She doesn't move at all.

"How are we going to do this?" he asks.

The men lower the gurney to the ground. The gloved officer tries again to move her, without success. The tall officer moves in and begins pulling her out using a great deal of force. He holds her by her wrists as her body falls onto the ground, just outside the car. Another officer moves in to help, grabbing her by the jeans that are wound around her calf. Finally, they place her body on the gurney. There is no special care taken, no tenderness, or respect. I'm not sure what I expected to see, but it wasn't this. I realize once again that I need to remind myself to breathe.

"She's *all* marked up. Walk over this way Chief . . . look at this . . . " The camera zooms in on a scratch on my mother's neck.

"You tell them, whoever does the autopsy, they sure better check to see if there's a piece of fingernail in that scratch mark." The camera pans again, zooming in on three dark holes in her chest.

"What's that there in the middle of her chest?"

"Looks like a .22." The gloved officer sticks a finger inside one of the holes and digs around, looking for a bullet.

"There's only one way to figure this out, so let's get going."

They cover her upper body with a thin, paper-like sheet, then toss a red blanket over the rest of her body. The gurney is raised, and they roll her out of the camera's view. The time is 12:05 p.m.

Fuck.

I WANT MY MOMMY

The screen goes gray at 48.06. I let it run for a few seconds more before a new video pops up on the screen. It is a six-year-old boy being questioned by a Black female police officer in uniform. I lean in close. Yes, that's me. Why is this at the end of the crime scene video? My mind swirls. Was it attached by mistake?

I am wearing a blue tank top and look visibly nervous; shaken. The video is time-stamped at 9:51 a.m. 8.25.87, two days after my mother was found dead. The police officer and I are sitting side by side in metal chairs, facing the camera.

"Your dad's gonna step outside, and we're gonna make a video. Is that ok," she asks.

I nod, still visibly shaken. My mother just died. My mother was *killed*. What the hell? Why are they questioning such a small boy? Why are they questioning *me*? It gives me chills and at the same time fills me with rage. I want to reach into the screen and grab that little boy.

"Can you tell me your name?" she asks, leaning in. "What's your name?"

I move away and look down, peering up at her from the tops of my eyes. My posture is slumped, and I am clearly uncomfortable. I fiddle with a tissue, and it falls out of my hands and onto the floor. The officer leans in even more as she picks up the tissue and hands it to me.

"Reggie," I answer. My voice is so small.

"Reggie, how old are you?"

"Six."

"Six years old. You're a big boy."

No, no I'm not a big boy. I am six years old. And my mother is dead. She is trying to gain my trust, but I continue to lean away from her, my bottom as far over on the chair as it can get without me falling off.

"Do you go to school? Where do you go to school?" she asks. I see that she has become aware of how uncomfortable I am, and her questions take on a faster pace.

"Holy Ghost," I say, in the tiniest voice.

"Holy Ghost! You enjoy going to school over there? Got a lot of friends?" she asks. More rapid-fire questioning. She has turned her body toward me now, still leaning in. I begin to feel claustrophobic as I watch the video, once again trapped by a situation completely out of my control.

"You got a lot of friends over there?" she repeats.

"Yeah," I say, my voice trailing off.

"Name some of your friends," she says. This is beginning to feel like an interrogation. The tension is palpable. She must be trying to establish my ability to recall information.

I shake my head no.

"You don't know your friends?"

I shake my head again.

"Okay," she relents.

I can tell that she's becoming frustrated. I guess I'm not coop-
erating as she hoped. Her hands are clasped together tightly, and
she is wringing her fingers.

"What kind of toys do you like to play with?"

I shrug my shoulders.

"You don't know what kind of toys you like to play with?" she
asks again.

I shrug again.

"What kind of bicycle do you have? Do you have a bicycle?"

The tension is building. I am not giving her what she wants
or needs.

"A BMX," I answer.

"Wow, I bet you go fast on that, huh? Do you go fast?"

I nod.

"Okay . . . what else you got? Do you have a toy gun?"

I nod.

"Last night I saw that you had a robe on. A thing you put on
over your shirt. That was neat. Did you get that for Christmas?"

Where in the world is she going with this?

"My daddy bought it," I answer.

"Your daddy bought it? Boy, I bet you was happy when he
bought you that."

I nod.

"What you like to watch on TV?"

I feel like I know where she's going with this now. She is
maneuvering the questions toward the night of my mother's
murder.

"Cartoons," I say.

"You know, I have a ten-year-old little boy. He likes to watch cartoons, too." She is still trying to gain trust. Who knows if she even had a ten-year-old boy.

"What else you like to do?"

"Play baseball," I answer, my voice cracking. She goes in for the kill.

"What'd you do Saturday?"

"Watched TV."

"How long did you watch TV?"

How in the world would a six-year-old know the specific amount of time he watched TV? I remain quiet.

"Did you go anywhere Saturday?"

I shake my head no.

"Do you know when Saturday was?"

I shake my head no.

"You don't? Did you go to church Sunday?"

I shake my head no.

"You didn't go to church Sunday? Okay the day before Sunday, what did you do?"

I just said I didn't know when Saturday was. How was I supposed to know when Sunday was if I didn't know the day *before* Sunday? I probably didn't even know the days of the week at this age.

"I think I was probably playing my games," I answered.

"Did you go ride anywhere?"

I shake my head no.

"You didn't leave the house at all the day before Sunday?"

I shake my head no.

"Well, what else did you do?" Her voice heightens and her frustration shows.

"Just play."

"You didn't go to the mall?"

I shook my head yes.

"You *did* go to the mall?"

I shook my head yes.

"Who took you to the mall?"

I began to cry.

"I want my daddy. . . I want my daddy. . . I want my daddy," I cry, covering my face with my tiny hand. She rubs my back. "I want my daddy now."

"Okay stop crying. We'll get him for you," she says, as she tries to calm me down. My crying becomes loud, and inconsolable. She's done enough damage, and I'm done answering her questions.

"I want my daddy. I want you to go get him *now*," I say.

I try to stand up and she puts her hand on my shoulder, pushing me back down in the chair. She stands and walks out of view, and I hear her saying, "Okay, stop that crying." She walks back into the frame and sits down, placing her hand on my knee. I recoil from her touch.

"Okay, I just need to ask you one more thing and then I'll go get him."

No. Not okay. My cries intensify.

"I want my daddy. I want my daddy now."

Then, I hear myself say "I want my mommy!"

She relents and tries to hug me. I get up and walk toward the camera, most likely headed for the door. My daddy is on the other side of that door. The screen goes gray. This interrogation accomplished nothing more than reveal my deep suffering and need for my mother.

I want my mommy.

It was a slip, I think. I knew she was gone.

PART FOUR

THE TRIAL

CIGARETTE BUTT

The murder charges brought against my father all stemmed from a cigarette butt. On June 21st, 2019, a grand jury handed down an indictment and issued arrest warrants for my father and a man named Jessie Lee Jones. Hammond Police Chief said that new technology applied to old evidence led to this breakthrough in my mother's case.

In 1987, a cigarette butt was taken into evidence. The cigarette was found inside the car near my mother's dead body. Forensic testing was limited in 1987, so nothing ever came of this particular piece of evidence. I am unaware of what prompted the Hammond Police Department to reopen my mother's investigation, but one of their first actions was to test possible saliva remains on the cigarette butt for DNA.

The police ran the results through CODIS (Combined DNA Index System). CODIS is a computer software program that operates local, state, and national databases of DNA profiles from convicted offenders, unsolved crime scene evidence, and missing persons. A positive hit came back indicating DNA from a man whose identical twin brother had been part of the original investigation. Being an identical twin meant that the two men shared the same DNA. This identical twin was Jessie Lee Jones.

Jones was already in the system for various criminal offenses but wasn't currently incarcerated. Hammond police detectives questioned Jones in 1987 after my mother was found, but he repeatedly claimed he "knew nothing." Based on the positive hit in CODIS, the cigarette butt placed Jessie Lee Jones at the scene, and he was now being considered a suspect in the murder of my mother. In 2019 Hammond police detectives located Jessie Lee Jones living under a bridge in Atlanta. Jail records show that Jones was booked into the Tangipahoa Parish Jail in Amite City, Louisiana at 4:25 p.m. on June 27th, 2019.

He was charged with Second-Degree Murder and Conspiracy.

According to court records, Jones met with his attorney and family members on Thursday, November 14th, 2019, after which he agreed to a "video recorded statement—a narrative supplemental—regarding additional details of the alleged crime." Jones then "provided details as to his recollection of the events in which he took part on the evening of August 22nd, 1987, the night before Selonia Reed's body was found."

It turns out that Jessie Lee Jones's story had changed drastically since 1987.

"Jones detailed colluding with Reginald Reed Sr. for the transport of Selonia Reed's car and her deceased body to the John's Curb Market in Hammond where she would later be discovered by police."

Jones's story had changed from "knew nothing" to collusion. How could he be trusted? He either "knew nothing," or he colluded. The following is taken from the Supplemental Narrative dated November 14, 2019:

"Jones detailed how he drove a grey Ford Crown Victoria to pick up Reed from the John's Curb Market the night before Selonia Reed's body was discovered. He said Reed brought him the car and parked it on the street near his (Jones's) sister's house. He said Reed had previously discussed with him where to pick him up. Jones followed through and drove to the location during the nighttime hours. He observed Reginald Reed exiting Selonia's blue Chevy Sprint parked next to John's Curb Market. He saw Reed dressed in dark colored clothing and wearing brown work gloves. Jones walked around to the passenger side of Selonia's car and observed her sitting in the passenger seat. He said her eyes were open and believed she had been crying. She was fully clothed, and he noticed blood coming from her nose. He initially said he was unsure if she was deceased or not, but later in the interview confirmed Selonia Reed was deceased at the time he observed her in the car. Jones also told how Reginald Reed approached him a few days before Selonia's body was discovered and asked him to make his wife (Selonia Reed) disappear. He said Reginald Reed later offered him $50,000 for the help."

The following is taken from Jones' original statement in 1987:

Detective: "Did he offer you any money?"

Jones: "No, he ain't. He ain't offered me nothin'."

Detective: "Did he ever say anything to you about any money?"

Jones: "No."

His story about the car had changed drastically as well.

Detective: "Did he ask you anything about driving his car?"

Jones: "No. He ain't said nothin' about driving no car."

The whole scenario feels strategic to me. A hearing was held on Thursday, November 7th, 2019, to suppress a motion against my father. The Assistant District Attorney was approached by Jones's attorney:

"At the conclusion of the hearing, the Assistant District Attorney was approached by Jones's attorney in which he requested a meeting with Jones, Jones's family, and the prosecuting authority. This was allegedly to provide additional information in regard to the ongoing criminal matter. The District Attorney complied with the request and set the meeting for November 14th, 2019."

Jones was doing everything he could to *comply* with detectives and provide information that would lead to a lesser charge—and therefore a lesser sentence—for himself. He met with his lawyer and family *before* providing the supplemental narrative. If Jones confessed to collusion or conspiracy, claiming he simply drove a car to pick up my father, he would be charged as an *accessory* to murder. This meant that it would benefit Jones to provide the supplemental narrative to Hammond detectives.

I am sure that his attorney and family advised him to do so. Accessory to Murder versus Second-Degree Murder? That's a no-brainer.

Of course, Jones portrayed himself as nothing more than the driver. He told police that he was afraid of my father, and acted as he did because he was afraid for his life. He was doing anything and everything he could to strike a deal with the District

Attorney and get a lesser charge and reduced sentence. Jones would continue to stay in contact with the District Attorney, and details continued to unfold.

TRIAL DAY 1

The trial was set to begin on Monday, November 14th, 2023. This was thirty-six years, two months, and twenty-two days after the murder of my mother. I woke up that morning feeling indifferent. So much time had passed, with so many delays for justice. My life had been in a holding pattern for so long that I just wanted this part to be over.

The trial was being held in Amite City, Louisianna, about 20 miles North of Hammond. Day 1 had been jury selection; today we would begin the long road of trial and testimony. I left my hotel at 7:30 a.m., heading to my childhood home to pick up my father. He was waiting on the small front porch, sharply dressed in a suit and tie. We exchanged a few words; nothing too deep. We stopped at McDonald's for coffee and a breakfast sandwich.

Looking back, there are so many things I should have said during that 20-minute drive, and so many questions I should have asked. I should have told him how this had affected me and my life, and how I knew that it would continue to do so long after the verdict was read. I should have told my father how my life felt like collateral damage in all that had happened within our family. I should have told him that I didn't deserve any of it. But those words didn't come. It felt more appropriate to simply ride together in the quiet of the morning, just sitting next to one another in this shared space.

We arrived on time and walked together through the large double doors. It was surreal; we knew almost every person working in the courthouse that day. Small towns, I guess. People know one another. The man working the metal detector greeted us.

"Hey, Mr. Reed! Hey, Lil' Reggie!"

We were treated more like local celebrities than a man on trial for murder and his son. We exchanged smiles, handshakes, hugs, and pats on the back. As we entered the courtroom, jury selection was already underway. I noticed that the assistant to the prosecutor was a former classmate of mine from Holy Ghost. Again, surreal. So many connections.

In the end, the jury was comprised of one Black male, two Black females, and a mix of nine White men and women. Most were middle-aged or older except for the two Black females who appeared to be in their twenties. It is hard to know whether a jury is favorable to your side of the case until things really get going. We didn't spend much time discussing or debating the jurors with my father's defense team. It was what it was, and we would have to move forward.

The courtroom was cold, almost freezing. I wished I had worn more layers. My body felt stiff and shaky, and I just didn't feel like myself. The stress was beginning to set in as I looked around the packed courtroom. There were nine people from my mother's side of the family sitting behind the prosecution, most notably my two aunts—my mother's sisters. None of them wanted to make eye contact with me. I hadn't spoken to either of them since I was very young. They hated my father, and I was shrapnel.

This made me lose any possibility of a relationship with them long ago.

Opening statements began. The prosecution painted my father as "a mastermind who preyed on the weak." They told the jury my father "kept close to those in power so he would never be considered a suspect in the murder." The defense told the jury my father was "caught up in a nightmare where his wife had been killed, and now 35 years later *his* life is in jeopardy." She reminded the jury that the crime had been fully investigated in 1987 and that my father was never charged. He had lived his entire life in Hammond. Now, thirty-five years later he was being accused and charged with murder because of a cigarette butt that didn't even match his DNA. The DNA evidence belonged to the co-defendant who was currently wheeling and dealing with the prosecution.

This was the literal definition of a nightmare.

The prosecution called its first witness, an officer from the Hammond Police Department who was part of my mother's case in 1987. He answered questions about the crime scene and about the friend my mother was with the night she was murdered. He testified that during questioning this female friend admitted to him that she would often "cover" for my mother if she wanted to do something or go somewhere without my father knowing. The officer confirmed, however, that the female friend did not cover for my mother on the night of the murder.

The officer's testimony didn't contain anything earth-shattering, although it did plant the seed that my mother and father may not have had the perfect relationship. But who does? A rough marriage doesn't implicate murder.

The second witness was another Hammond Police Department detective who also worked on my mother's original case. He was asked to sketch the location of the crime scene, after which the prosecution played the entire 53-minute video of the crime scene footage for the courtroom. You could have heard a pin drop as the video played. Having seen it before, I looked around the courtroom, observing everyone. My aunts were crying, even sobbing at times. People were sitting straight up, leaning in, eyes glued to the grainy video.

An ice-cold chill ran through me. This felt bad—really bad. It's hard not to want someone, anyone, to pay for what they were seeing. I began to worry, my anxiety becoming almost unbearable. There was no way this video wouldn't negatively impact my father's case. These people needed someone to blame for the horrors they were seeing and hearing, and in the absence of any other suspects, I feared they would decide then and there that my father was guilty.

The video ended and the prosecutor handed the officer a bag of evidence, asking him to open it in front of the courtroom. He was given a pair of latex gloves and some scissors. He stood, walked to a table in front of the jury box, and began opening each smaller bag within the large evidence bag. As he opened each one, he was asked to describe the item within.

"A toy police car," he began.

This must have been mine, although I don't have any memory of it. The tiny car solicited cries from my aunts, a painful reminder I suppose that she was taken from me and me from her. I choked up, too. The prosecution knew it was there and that it would elicit powerful emotions from everyone. That is why it was the first bag to be opened.

Next, he unbagged a small car vacuum which was seen in the crime scene video. It was on the floorboard where my mother's legs lay, lifeless. Third, a small bouncy ball. Another reminder of me. More cries, as the officer continued with the display.

A tissue.

A small notebook.

A photo of me. So many reminders of me. More sobs.

A little wallet.

My mother's driver's license.

Finally, the umbrella that was found in my mother's vagina.

The cries and sobs became loud once again. Who would do such a sick thing? Why would someone want to hurt my mother so badly? I had seen it in the video, but seeing it in person, held up like this, shook me in a way that I was not expecting. I fought back the urge to vomit.

Breathe, Reggie. Breathe . . .

I could taste bile in the back of my throat, hot and acidic. My eyes burned and watered. I swallowed hard and willed myself not to wretch. I was not expecting the next items. I fought off the intense urge to flee as the detective began pulling the items from the bag.

It was her clothing. First, my mother's underwear. It was covered in old, dried blood.

My heart shattered. I could physically feel it burst into pieces within my chest, settling heavy and sending shockwaves throughout my body. One of my aunts ran out of the courtroom in tears. Everything in me wanted to follow her, to get out of there, too. I didn't want to see these things. I didn't know if I could handle much more.

Next was her ivory-colored bra, now yellowed by time and covered in splatters of brown dried blood.

The entire courtroom burst with emotion. The crime scene video, her personal items, and now the clothing she wore while being murdered was just too much. I cannot recall ever feeling as overwhelmed as I did at this moment. The depths of sadness I was feeling were incomprehensible. I had to hover; being present and solidly within my body was too painful. I stayed that way, taking in bits and pieces from this point on. I couldn't focus, nor did I want to.

I wanted out.

I did not want to feel.

I don't know how much time passed or what other items were revealed. I was in a fog of self-preservation. I was so cold. Still, so cold. The judge called a recess after the detective finished. Everyone needed a break. I ran to the restroom and could no longer hold back. Afterward, I slid down the wall of the stall, put my head between my legs, and wept. This is only day one.

Breathe, Reggie. Breathe . . .

I don't know how long I remained on the floor of that tiny stall. At last, my head stopped spinning. I stood and gathered myself as best I could. I splashed cold water on my face, rinsed my mouth out, and headed back to the courtroom. It was nearing five o'clock by this time. *Surely there couldn't be much more today,* I hoped.

The final witness was the forensic pathologist who performed my mother's autopsy. He was now a much older man, in his late seventies if I had to guess. He was asked a variety of questions by both the defense and the prosecution. His testimony was marked with personal bias. When either side would ask him to describe the condition of my mother's body his replies were filled with unnecessary emotion and drama.

"Selonia Reed experienced GREAT PAIN," he said, his voice so loud it bordered on yelling.

The defense objected and the judge warned him to "please just state the facts." Despite being admonished by the Judge, he continued as before.

"She was STABBED OVER AND OVER AGAIN," he fairly screamed, this time louder than the last.

Another objection. Another warning from the judge.

"Her face was DESTROYED, MUTILATED beyond recognition."

I could see that his emotional rhetoric was impacting the jury. He had their full attention, and when he yelled, they retracted in their seats, stunned by the ferocity of his words. *This is not good,* I thought. The defense requested to approach the bench and speak with the judge. A short recess was called, after which the jury was told not to consider the pathologist's testimony. They were asked to completely disregard everything he said on the stand and instructed to use only the autopsy report when discussing this portion of the case.

That's a win, I thought. But then again, how does one completely disregard something they saw and heard? Things cannot be unheard or unseen; we're all human.

The day ended and everyone gathered their things and filed out of the courtroom. I've never been so ready for something to be over in my life. On the way out, my father and I were greeted by more people we knew from back in the neighborhood. We exchanged more handshakes, more pats on the back, and more professions of shock and surprise that this was happening to us after all these years. I overheard a conversation between two top officials who worked on my mother's case.

"Thirty-five years later? Total bullshit."

I couldn't agree more. Total bullshit.

The drive home was quiet. We were both exhausted and unable to attempt even small talk. I had absolutely nothing to say. I was empty—numb. The image of my mother's clothes kept running in a loop through my mind. The sadness set in, and tears welled in my eyes. I fought them back so as not to upset my father. We drove up the tiny gravel driveway and just sat for a moment. We looked at one another and my father got out, walking into the house without saying a word.

Total bullshit, I thought. Total bullshit.

COLOGNE

Our sense of smell is powerful and capable of eliciting a plethora of memories and emotions. I smelled my father's cologne as he got into my car that first morning of the trial. It was a warm, familiar smell with a hint of spice. It was comforting, something that I had smelled for decades. He had always worn the same scent. I breathed it in that first morning, my heart racing and stomach churning for what the day ahead held.

But, for a moment, I was calm. My head stopped spinning. My heartbeat slowed. My stomach eased. My hands, held in tight fists, softened. That smell—his smell—made me feel for just a moment that everything was going to be okay. Hours later when my father got out of the car after that first day of the trial, his scent lingered.

I reached over and touched the passenger seat where he had been, transferring the familiar smell to my hand. I sat for a long time, my hands over my face, and breathed in the smell of his cologne. The scent flooded my mind with memories of the past. I recalled watching my father dress in the mornings before driving me to school. He would carefully brush his hair and straighten his collar, bending down slightly to look in the mirror. The last step in his routine was always cologne. Sometimes he would spray it against his neck. Sometimes he would spray it on his hands and pat it against his face like aftershave. It was an ever-present smell—*his* smell.

Sitting there that evening, my mind spinning with the images from the trial, the smell, and all its bound-up memories unleashed the torrent of tears I had been desperately holding back. I sobbed, beating my hand against the steering wheel. My body shook and tightened. Just as I wiped away tears, more came.

What if things don't go the way we hope, and I never again get to smell the scent of my father's cologne? Where will all the bound-up memories go? Will they be lost, dissipated into thin air as if they never existed? What or who would I be if there were no memories? All my memories included him. What if I lose him? What if it's all lost? Who would *I* be without *him*? What if I lose both my mother *and* my father? If that happens, I will truly be alone.

It feels so cruel.

The memories won't matter, then. Who would I share them with?

The reality of this hit me harder than I ever expected. All of this over the smell of his cologne. I wanted to bottle it up along with the memories and hide it away for safekeeping, untouched by the outcome of the trial. I cried all the way back to my hotel. The car was filled with a mixture of his cologne and the damp Louisiana night air. I parked and reached over once again—this time with both hands—and touched the spot where his neck had rested against the back of the seat. Again, the scent absorbed into my skin.

I lay in bed that night with my hands curled under my chin like a child, the comforting smell of my father lulling me to sleep.

TRIAL DAY 2

Here we go again.

My father was once again waiting on the porch. We stopped for coffee and breakfast sandwiches from McDonald's, then drove the 20 miles to Amite City, parked, and entered the courthouse. I wondered how many days this routine would go on. It was rumored that this may be the longest trial in the history of the parish. My stomach churned at the thought. I already missed my wife and son. This was only day two, and already I felt exhausted and completely wrung out. What if this went on for weeks? Months?

The courtroom was packed with standing room only on day two. The rumor mill was in full swing, and all sorts of people had come, trying to get any information they could. It was just as cold in the courtroom as it had been the day before. I took my seat toward the back and mentally prepared myself. I never again wanted to feel like I had the day before; helpless, panicked, physically ill. I was determined to stay in control of my emotions on day two. It helped that today my uncles—my father's brothers—and my best friend Quentin had joined me in the courtroom. I felt supported and better able to handle whatever the day may bring.

The first witness was my mother's close female friend. She was covered nearly head to toe in black. She wore a black scarf covering her neck, a mask from her chin to just below her eyes, and a head wrap that went all the way down to her eyebrows. All that was visible were her eyes. It was unsettling. Did she not want to be recognized? Were these COVID-19 precautions? I thought the whole thing was strange, and not a great way to start the second day.

This was the same woman that the Hammond police officer testified would often "cover" for my mother if she didn't want my father to know her whereabouts. She answered a variety of questions from both the defense and prosecution. Throughout her testimony, I could hear my aunts—my mother's sisters— audibly huff and puff. At one point the judge stopped the witness mid-sentence and warned my aunts that if they continued, they would be asked to leave the courtroom for the remainder of the day.

Emotions were running hot and high, and this was only the first witness.

This witness was notable because she was adding information to her testimony that wasn't in the original report from 1987. She embellished, claiming that my father called her and threatened her. None of this was in the original report she gave the day after my mother's body was found.

The defense objected repeatedly as she added details, played up stories, and tried to incriminate my father. The objections were all sustained, but the jury still heard the words. Doubt had been introduced. Was she telling the truth *now*, or was she telling the truth back in 1987? Her testimony wasn't a total loss for our side. She appeared unreliable at best, and we hoped the jury would recognize and take note of her inconsistencies.

The next witness was the Hammond Chief of Police in 1987. The first issue he addressed was a scratch found on my father's neck when he was brought in for questioning. The prosecution pulled up the photos, and the officer was asked to recount my father's explanation of the scratch. He said that "at first (my father) said the scratch was from a neighborhood dog, then later said it was a scratch from playing basketball with friends in the neighborhood." It was nothing really, probably 2-inches in length. No one would have even noticed this type of scratch had they not been investigating a murder. It was superficial, and the skin wasn't broken; however, my father's changing story? That could be a problem.

Next, the questioning turned to the condition of the house when the police came to look a few days after my mother's body had been found. The officer testified that the house was "clean and the carpet freshly vacuumed." He said he bent down, ran his hands along the carpet, and found a small necklace clasp. He claimed that when he did so my father's face turned "white as a ghost."

Our house would have been full of people at this time, with family members stopping by to offer their condolences and neighbors bringing food. That could have been anyone's necklace clasp. It could also have been my mother's, randomly lost in the house. A necklace clasp found on the carpet doesn't mean my father murdered my mother. It doesn't mean anything. It's just a broken necklace clasp. The Chief's insistence that my father's face turned "white as a ghost" looked like guilt on my father's part. This was a total stretch, but enough to possibly sway the jury into agreeing with the officer.

The next witness was the mall security guard from 1987. He was asked if he saw my father, my mother, and me at the mall on the afternoon of August 22nd. He testified that he didn't see my father, only my mother and me; but added that this did not mean my father was not there. There were no further questions, and the defense let that last statement settle in with the jury.

The judge, a heavy-set red-faced man, called a recess after the security guard's testimony. I was shocked by his nonchalance. His tone and demeanor said he didn't want to be here, and certainly didn't want to be presiding over this case. Whether that was because he thought this was total bullshit after 35 years or if he just truly didn't care either way, it was hard to know.

During recess, my father and I were approached in the parking lot by a male cousin from my mother's side of the family. He was hopped up on the emotions of the day, becoming instantly aggressive and screaming at my father "I should beat your ass!" When we turned to face him, he screamed "Don't you look at me! I'm gonna beat your ass!"

What in the actual hell, I thought. *Are we going to have to fight off this kid right here in the parking lot, on top of everything else?* The young man was erratic and unstable. He bobbed and weaved, even lunged toward us, undoubtedly fueled by the emotions of my mother's sisters. When I think about it now, I'm sure he, too, was just hurting. Maybe he felt helpless and confused, not knowing what to do with all the emotion surrounding him. Maybe he was acting out of sheer pain.

I chose to view him as harmless, a little dog with a loud bark.

After the recess, the judge made a statement to the court. Now appearing even more red-faced than before he warned everyone that "if any further drama ensues, people may be asked to leave the courtroom for the remainder of the day, or worse, the remainder of the trial." In other words, *you people better keep your shit together*. At last, he was showing *some* emotion.

The first witness was a woman from the neighborhood. She testified that on the afternoon of August 22nd she was driving to the mall and my mother was driving behind her. She further testified that she did not see my father in the passenger seat. The defense pounced on this, as it was in direct contradiction to her statement in 1987. Back then, she stated that *she* was driving behind my mother, and didn't see my father in the passenger seat.

"Besides the fact that your testimony does not match that of your statement from 1987, how could you identify that Mr. Reed was not in the car driving behind you?" the defense asked.

She went on to say that when she looked in her rear-view mirror, she did not see my father in the car. Again, the defense let that settle in the minds of the jury. *Unreliable at best once again,* I thought. Shifting statements and perfect vision through a rear-view mirror? Clearly, this didn't come close to incriminating my father who had already stated that we went to the mall as a family that afternoon.

At this point, I felt like the day was a win for us. Unreliable witness testimony from the mall security guard, a random necklace clasp, and a contradictory rear-view testimony? None of it added up to anything substantial in my mind. None of it was comprised of any real evidence, certainly none that pointed to my father killing my mother.

The next witness entered the courtroom in shackles and wearing the prison orange of a man already incarcerated. The courtroom fell silent as he made his way up the center aisle and onto the witness stand. He had everyone's attention.

The man testified that my father and Jessie Lee Jones had been at his apartment discussing the murder of my mother. He could not recall a timeline or any other details, only that he had heard this discussion.

Damn. Not good. I relied on the fact that this was an incarcerated man, and the jury would deem him unreliable. I hoped so, at least. The defense had no questions, they just wanted him out of there. His mere presence was unsettling.

The final witness on day two was my mother's sister. The moment she took the stand she became emotional and continued to cry throughout her entire testimony. She testified that my father called her the morning after my mother hadn't come home and asked if she had spent the night at her house. She added that my father seemed "normal, calm, and unemotional." She, however, became more and more emotional, her cries turning to sobs.

I could see the jury perk up. No one likes to see someone in such an emotional state. It pulls at your emotions. The defense chose not to question her. Just like the previous witness, they wanted her off the stand as quickly as possible. I wasn't worried so much about what she said as I was about the emotional impact she may have had on the jury. After all, this was a woman who had lost her sister, and I was worried the jury might empathize with her.

Day two was long, but I was feeling good. Our defense team was feeling good as well. Not much added up on this day, and we left the courtroom feeling hopeful.

God, that felt good.

ALARM CLOCK

The alarm clock blared. I hadn't expected to sleep so heavily, assuming instead that I would wake well before the set time. The exhaustion of the days, weeks, months, years, and decades must be catching up with me.

The sound of the alarm had startled me, and somehow hit differently on this day. I wasn't waking up for a normal day of work, running errands, and being a husband and parent; I was waking up to take my father to day three of a trial that would decide whether he spent the rest of his life behind bars for the murder of my mother. The stakes were as high as they could be. That alarm hit differently.

I settled myself and smelled my hands, searching for the comfort of my father's cologne. The sent was gone—completely gone. Not a trace of it remained. I smelled the pillow just in case. Nothing. Wanting to cry, I pulled myself out of bed and went through the motions of preparing for the day. I felt exhausted despite sleeping through the night, and I would have given anything to climb back into the bed and pull the sheets over my head. I longed to hide from the world; to hit the pause button.

I'm not ready. I'm not ready. I tried everything I could think of to calm down. I face-timed my wife and son, a brief time of reprieve where I looked into their faces and my thoughts and anxiety settled. Before long, it was time to go. Time to pick up my father. Time to kick the can. Keep things moving. *Kick the can.*

I pulled into the driveway of my childhood home. My dad was ready, waiting for me on the small front porch. He looked so tired. His posture, once upright and tight with confidence now seemed bent and curved under the weight of his circumstances. He walked to the car slowly and let out a deep exhausted sigh as he sat beside me. My mind started to race, and my vision became blurry. My chest tightened. I felt like I was going a million miles per hour while simultaneously frozen in place. I couldn't move.

"Son . . . ?"

I could hear my father's voice, but it felt so far away. I couldn't speak. *Say something, Reggie.* My thoughts blistered in my head. Say something . . .

I want to grab you around the neck and pull you close, and cry, and yell, and pound my fists on the steering wheel and tell you all the things I never had the courage to say. I want to tell you how much I love you, and how broken I will be if they take you away from me. I want to run away. I want to hide you somewhere where no one will ever find you, and we can be safe. I love you, I love you, I love you. I can't lose you too.

"You ready, son?" My father's voice jarred me back to the moment.

I am sweating, my stomach churning. I feel nauseous and confused. No, I'm not ready. I will never be ready. I just had a panic attack, a full-blown panic attack. I will never again wake up without thinking of this day.

Or maybe I will.

Maybe it is true that time heals some wounds. Perhaps one day the alarm will sound, and I will get up knowing that this day is tucked away in a safe place, no longer hovering over me.

But that is not today.

TRIAL DAY 3

The State Farm agent who issued my mother's life insurance policies was the first witness on day three. He testified that my father took out several life insurance policies on my mother in the year leading up to her murder. He went on to add that he allowed my father to sign the policies without my mother being present. He said he spoke to my mother over the phone and accepted this as her signature.

The prosecution pounced.

The agent could not be sure that he *actually* spoke to my mother, only that he spoke to a woman claiming to be my mother. He referenced another call that he had with my mother in which the woman knew details that only my mother would know. This led him to believe he was speaking with her when she called to approve the life insurance policies. He went on to say that he never doubted that he spoke to my mother until after her murder. It was a small town. Everyone knew everyone.

"This was just how business was done back in 1987," he said.

This testimony was problematic for us. My father had taken out several life insurance policies over the year leading up to my mother's death totaling approximately $750,000. Even more problematic was the fact that he had taken out one of these policies just weeks before her murder. *Shit*, I thought. *This doesn't look good*. I began to feel the familiar pangs of panic rising in my chest. *No. No. No. Not again.* I clenched my cold fists to distract myself from the rising anxiety.

The prosecution presented the policies to the jury. It was pin-drop silent for the next twenty minutes as they passed each one around. Time felt frozen—paused. I watched as each member of the jury read over the policies. I felt myself trying to go numb again and fought to stay present in the moment. I wanted to see their faces. I wanted to discern their thoughts.

Finally, it's over, I thought.

But it wasn't.

The next witness was a First Circuit Court of Appeals Judge who had also been the attorney representing State Farm in 1987. This woman had been the lead attorney investigating the life insurance claims, and was tasked with determining whether the policies would be paid to my father after my mother's murder. She had been given access to everything collected by the Hammond Police Department and had deposed my father on several occasions.

The prosecution noted that she had asked my father about a necklace my mother always wore. They were trying to tie this to the clasp found on the carpet. This was a huge stretch. How would this woman know about a necklace my mother wore? There were definite holes in her testimony, but I worried that it wouldn't matter. I worried that the jury would see this very successful judge on the stand and take her word as the gospel truth. As the prosecution wrapped up, she testified that at the end of her investigation, State Farm and my father had come to a resolution.

"No further questions," the prosecution said.

Without warning the witness blurted, "Don't y'all want to know what the resolution was?"

Then, she laughed. She was laughing. Laughing! *What the hell,* I thought. She's a judge! Surely, she knows better than to blurt something out after the questioning has ended. What in the hell was she trying to do? Thankfully, the judge called a recess for lunch.

The defense requested a mistrial after recess, citing the outburst of the former State Farm agent. The defense argued that her words were "leading", and the outburst was "a breach of process." This type of misconduct could sway the jury. The judge denied the request.

Jessie Lee Jones was called to the stand next. He, too, wore prison orange. He was light-skinned and bald and looked much older than I expected. He began his testimony by explaining how he knew my mother. He said that she had helped him cash his checks at the bank when he didn't have an ID, describing her as "a very nice woman." He also said that he knew my father from the neighborhood and expressed that he was afraid of him.

His speech was hard to understand, and if I didn't know better would have thought he had been drinking heavily. He testified that my father approached him about "knocking someone off for $50,000." Later, he claimed my father came to him and asked him specifically to "knock off his wife."

He denied agreeing to knock off my mother.

His story was that my father asked him to help, and he agreed because he feared for his own life. He told the court that my father orchestrated everything, claiming that my father left a car for him to use to pick him up from the gas station where my mother had been found. He said he pulled up to the scene and saw my mother in her car, adding that it "looked like she had been crying" but that he wasn't sure whether she was dead at this point.

It is important to note that when Jessie Lee Jones was questioned in 1987, he offered no information—zero. In 1987 Jessie Lee Jones "didn't know nothing." This changed in 2019 when the cigarette butt was tested, and the case reopened. Now, he wanted to talk, and he offered up this story that painted him as a man acting out of fear.

The prosecution made it clear that Jones was "here today to testify against (my father) in exchange for a deal."

"Why are you here today, Mr. Jones?" the prosecution asked.

"I'm here to clear my name and to get a five-year deal. And clear my name," Jones replied.

He was just a man living under a bridge who wanted that lesser sentence of accessory to murder. I don't think he truly cared about clearing his name. His eyes were solely focused on that plea deal.

Cross-examination by the defense was confrontational, and Jones was combative in his responses. The defense discredited everything he testified to, citing his original statement from 1987. He pointed out his shifting narrative on the stand and reminded the jury that in his original statement Jones "knew nothing." The defense brought up another murder that Jones had been associated with and served time for; however, the prosecution quickly objected.

At this point, Jones began coughing uncontrollably on the stand. The bailiff brought him water, but to no avail. The coughing fit only intensified. The courtroom was silent other than the low, deep, uncontrollable coughing of the witness. Jones tried to speak but could not.

This went on for what felt like hours. He would catch his breath, only to begin coughing again. The judge was finally forced to call a recess.

My uncles, father, and I went to lunch together. Lunch had become a time that we all looked forward to; an opportunity to spend time together under these terrible circumstances. We always said a prayer before eating, asking God to reveal the truth and bring justice for my mother. We begged God to release my father from this nightmare. We ate and talked as if this were just a normal lunch. There was little talk of the trial; we all needed this break.

I was acutely aware of my father during these lunches. I could see he was trying to steer the conversation away from himself. He didn't want to be the center of attention. We talked about old times. My father barely ate, just picking at his food. I could tell he was thinking, and processing. He looked bone tired. He did his best to participate in the conversation, but I knew that his mind was somewhere else. I couldn't blame him, because mine was, too.

While we sat eating lunch the prosecution was offering Jessie Lee Jones a deal. The defense had informed us ahead of time that this may happen. Upon returning from recess, we were told that Jones accepted the deal: Accessory to Murder: After the Fact.

An Accessory after the Fact is someone who assists someone who has committed a crime 1) after the person has committed the crime; 2) with knowledge that the person committed the crime; or 3) with the intent to help the person avoid arrest or punishment. His sentence was five years, which the prosecution argued he had already served. This meant that Jessie Lee Jones would walk out of the courtroom that day a free man.

Total bullshit.

Without Jones, the focus was now squarely on my father and how he alone was guilty of killing my mother. My stomach churned as I watched Jones leave the stand and walk down the center aisle and out the doors of the courtroom. I wanted to stand up and scream. I was furious, my whole body was shaking with the emotion. That man was free. I couldn't fathom it.

Everything in me said that Jones was lying. He *had* to be lying. What about the cigarette butt? *That's why we are all here today, isn't it?* If Jones just drove and picked up my father, how did the cigarette butt get there? Sure, he could have just flicked it out of the car window, but nothing in me believed that or anything else he said.

Next, the prosecution called a woman who was getting gas at the station near the carwash on the night my mother was killed. She testified that she was in her truck with her baby, and while writing a check for the gas observed a car pull by slowly and turn into the last bay of the carwash. She said it felt "suspicious," so she stayed in her vehicle for a moment to watch before going inside to pay for the gas. She continued, saying that she observed "two Black males in the vehicle who later both got out and walked around the car." She claimed it appeared as though they were looking for a place to "hide something" in the weeds along the back edge of the carwash. At this point, she claimed that she became suspicious enough to write down the license plate number of the vehicle.

The defense cross-examined. It was pointed out that her statement was handwritten in *black* ink, but the license plate number was written in *blue* ink, indicating that the license plate number wasn't written down at the same time as the initial statement. Perhaps it was added later, possibly at the suggestion of the police. To this, she responded, "Maybe the pen ran out of ink."

The defense asked, "Why, if you felt so suspicious of these two men, did you leave your baby in the car when you went in to pay for the gas?" She had no response.

No further questions.

Finally, the prosecution called the forensic expert who processed the DNA on the case. His testimony was short and to the point. He confirmed that all tests were done at his lab, and everything was done by the book. No questions from the defense.

The state rested.

There were deep sighs across the courtroom. It had been a long three days, and my father looked so tired. I felt exhausted, and totally wrung out. I can't imagine how deeply exhausted my father felt. I took account of the witnesses as I looked over my notes:

Day 1:

1. *Hammond police officer from 1987: Nothing substantial was offered other than my mother's friend admitted to him that she would often "cover" for my mother, but she had not done so the night of my mother's murder.*

2. *Hammond Detective from 1987: Crime scene video and the opening of evidence bags. This testimony did not fare well for us. It caused so much emotional upheaval from the cries and sobs of my aunts to clear emotional responses from the jury. This testimony worried me the most.*

3. *Forensic Pathologist who performed autopsy: THROWN OUT*

Day 2:

1. *My mother's friend: Covered from head to toe in black. Strange. Inconsistent. Said my dad called and threatened her after the murder, but this was not in her original account of events from 1987. She embellished on the stand. This was clear to me and appeared to be clear to the jury.*

2. *Hammond Chief of Police from 1987: Picture of scratch on my father's neck. My father first said it was from a neighborhood dog and later said it was from playing basketball with friends. This didn't look great for us. The scratch wasn't implicating but my father's change of story was problematic. Necklace clasp: At first this didn't seem like anything. It could have been anyone's necklace clasp BUT the State Farm Agent made the connection in her*

testimony which may lead the jury to believe this was indeed my mother's necklace clasp from a necklace that she "always" wore.

3. *Mall Security Guard: Only saw me and my mother at the mall but said that did not mean my father was not there.*

I felt good about some of the witnesses, but the crime scene video and evidence bags hung heavily over me. Then, there was the Jessie Lee Jones issue. Once a co-defendant, now a free man. In the absence of another person to consider as a suspect, I feared the jury would believe that my father acted alone and had, in fact, killed my mother. In their defense, I think that's just human nature. People don't like unsolved crimes. They need to feel like justice has been served.

We see this time and time again in the news where innocent people are finally exonerated after spending most of their lives in prison. Juries are made up of fallible human beings and can get it wrong sometimes, sending innocent people to prison—or worse—sentencing them to death.

———

Now that the prosecution had presented their witnesses and rested, it was our turn. The defense called their first witness, an incarcerated young man who had called the Hammond police tip line on September 5th, 2022. He had claimed to have information about the case and requested to speak to a detective. A detective traveled to the parish jail and interviewed the 22-year-old man.

The report written by the Hammond detective dated September 5th, 2022, states:

"[name redacted] said he shares a dorm with Jessie Lee Jones and about two weeks ago Jones told him about his involvement in a homicide several years ago. He said Jones did not mention the victim's name. He said Jones told him he hit the victim with a hammer and his brother stabbed the victim with an ice pick. He said Jones also told him they were to be paid thirty-five hundred dollars by the victim's husband. Jones told him the motive for killing the victim was she was having an affair with a White man. The young man told the court he called the tip line two more times with more information about the homicide but was not questioned again by detectives. Since [name redacted] never mentioned the name of the victim, Detective [name redacted] recognized the information was probably about the Selonia Reed homicide that happened in 1987 in Hammond, Louisianna. On September 6th, 2022, Detective [name redacted] notified the Assistant District Attorney's office, since the ADA is handling this case."

I read this report in the discovery before the trial, but seeing the young man on the stand and hearing him recount what Jones told him hit me like a freight train. So, Jones, a man who now walks free, precisely described my mother's injuries and the nature of her murder and told this witness of his involvement in the crime. Not only himself, but his brother as well—his twin brother—which makes the cigarette butt found at the scene an even more crucial piece of evidence against Jones.

This young man wasn't even born at the time of my mother's murder. In fact, he wouldn't be born for another fourteen years. There was no way he could have fabricated the details matching the fatal injuries to my mother. These details were only in the autopsy report.

CAUSE OF DEATH: Focal subarachnoid hemorrhage left parietal lobe. A fatal brain bleed in the left parietal lobe. The parietal lobe is underneath the crown of your skull, at the top rear of your head. This lines up with what Jones told the young man, saying "He (Jones) hit the victim with a hammer." Furthermore, his statement and testimony matched the nature of the stab wounds.

EVIDENCE OF INJURY: They [the stab wounds] measure .5 cm each with both extremes [ends] of the wounds appearing sharply angulated. An ice pick. This young man's testimony was the biggest piece of evidence thus far, and the prosecution did all they could to malign him as a witness.

"Do you remember me, Mr. Bevell," the prosecutor asked, fairly yelling the words. The young man looked confused. "I'm the one who put you in that orange suit you're wearing today, don't you remember?"

The young man was in prison, yes, but this didn't take away from the tip he provided to the police. The prosecution didn't want the jury to feel this way. They wanted them to see only the prison orange he was wearing and imagine the crime he must have committed to get there. I don't know why the tip from this young man was not taken more seriously. I will never know. But in my mind, Jessie Lee Jones got himself the deal of a lifetime.

The injustice is infuriating. Who knows if he will go back to living under a bridge or become incarcerated again at some point down the road. My only hope is that someday he will talk to someone else, and they will come forward with more information that could exonerate my father.

The defense called my uncle. He testified that I was never dropped off at my grandmother's home on the night my mother was murdered. My uncle was living there at the time. His testimony was short and sweet. The prosecution had no cross-examination, and day three of the trial ended.

We all—my dad, uncles, and me—gathered at the office of the Defense Attorney to discuss the trial thus far and prepare for the next day. It would be the final day of the trial. We talked about witnesses and strategy. We discussed the jurors and their reactions throughout the trial thus far, feeling confident that we had at least one juror on our side. This juror had been observed nodding in agreement when the defense poked holes in the prosecution's case, making them seem more empathetic to our case throughout the trial.

That's all we needed: One juror. One juror to say that the prosecution hadn't successfully proven without a shadow of a doubt that my father had killed my mother. One juror, and we would have a mistrial.

We discussed whether to put my father on the stand. By law, he was not required to testify. We went over the pros and cons, and in the end, we were all in agreement that it would be best for our case if my father did *not* take the stand. The reality of our situation was discussed openly and frankly. We all felt confident—especially about the one juror—but understood that this thing could go either way.

My father was upbeat, expressing several times that he felt good about the outcome. I, too, felt good—but *reservedly* good. I wasn't about to start celebrating anything until the verdict was read and it was all said and done.

The drive home hit me hard. What if this is it? What if we lose and I must drive home alone tomorrow—*alone*—my father taken away just as mother had been? It's difficult not to feel like a victim at times like this. I felt caught up in the middle with no escape. Stuck. I had no control over the outcome, and it could potentially go very badly for all of us; for *me*. I could lose another person that I loved. The only other parent I had could also be taken away.

I tried to make small talk with my father, but my mind was spinning. I was also dreading being called as a witness. I would be the final witness on the docket on day four. The final witness of the trial. I wondered if my nerves would get the best of me.

"It's gonna be alright," my father kept saying. "It's gonna be alright."

Was it though? I didn't share his eternal optimism. I felt like I had too much to lose. I suppose he couldn't let his mind wander like mine. Or maybe he did. Either way, he would never allow me to see or hear his greatest fears. He would stay strong for me—he always did. That was why our relationship worked all these years. He stayed strong.

I didn't sleep that night despite being utterly exhausted. I replayed everything from the three days prior in my mind and counted each witness as either a win or a loss for our side. I did this over and over again until the alarm blared.

I hadn't slept at all.

TRIAL DAY 4

Adrenaline did its job. I got out of bed, got ready, and made the trip to pick up my father. He was on the porch, as usual. We made our pit stop at McDonald's. I had zero appetite but made myself eat a hashbrown.

Most of my father's siblings were in the courtroom on this day, as was my best friend, Quentin. He had been there *every* day.

The trial opened with the man who had been the Mayor of Hammond at some point after my mother's murder. He testified to my father's character and involvement in the Hammond community. His testimony was short and to the point. He reiterated that my father was from a "well-respected family" and was "a good man and a good father."

The prosecution asked if my father had ever contributed financially to his mayoral campaigns. They were trying to make it look like a pay-off of sorts, a reason for why he should be saying these nice things about my father. The man denied ever taking any money from my father. He explained that my father helped with hanging signs, making phone calls, and knocking on doors, but that he never contributed financially.

I didn't feel like the prosecution's strategy was successful. What stood out to me were the words *well-respected family, good man, and good father*. I wondered if the jury took note of this, too. I hoped they had.

Next, the defense called the Hammond Bank president from 1987. There have been many rumors over the years that he and my mother were having an affair, and that he could have had something to do with her murder. He described my mother as a "sweet, hard-working lady from a great family." He added that he and my family attended the same church. The prosecutor pounced.

"Would you say Mr. Reed was a prominent figure in Hammond *because* the family had a lot of money?"

The former bank president responded by saying that, yes, my father was a prominent figure because he came from a well-known and well-respected family in the community. He went on to say that he had no knowledge of the Reed family's finances. There it was again: well-respected, well-known. *The prosecutor's attempts fell flat again,* I thought.

The next witness was our family attorney who handled the civil case over the life insurance policies that my father had taken out on my mother. The defense asked a few clarifying questions before the prosecution made their next attempt.

The prosecutor asked about the man's personal relationship with my father. The man responded that he was "unable to answer this because of attorney-client privilege." The prosecutor kept asking the same questions in a million different ways, but it all came down to nothing—the man was not going to willingly breach attorney-client privilege, nor could they make him. The attorneys were all asked to approach the bench where they engaged in a heated discussion for about 15 minutes before the judge called a short recess.

After the recess, my father waived his right to attorney-client privilege and the prosecution continued its questioning. It came down to the same responses from the two past witnesses. The attorney said that my father came from a "fine" family and that my father had "raised a fine young man." He sang my praises as he commented on how my father stepped up and filled the role of mother and father and that I had turned out to be an impressive man. He called me "Lil' Reggie," which made my heart skip a beat.

Lil' Reggie . . .

His testimony backfired on the prosecution. They should have let the attorney-client privilege issue rest. What they got was another testimony that painted my father as a good, well-respected man and father. None of that jived with the picture that the prosecution was trying to paint of my father being a cold-blooded killer. And not just any cold-blooded killer—the cold-blooded killer of his wife and the mother of his young son.

I don't often think in black and white, but to me, you can't be both types of people. Either you are the type of person who kills your wife, or you are a fine man in a well-respected family who chose to stay and raise his son when he could have easily left.

My uncle—my father's brother—testified next. He also testified that I wasn't dropped off at my grandmother's house the night my mother was murdered. He was emphatic on this point, saying that "there was no possible way that (I) was at my grandmother's house that night."

The prosecution didn't cross-examine since the jury had heard the same testimony from my other uncle. It was nearing time for lunch, and the attorneys for both sides debated whether the final witness—me—should testify before or after. They all agreed that I would take the stand after the lunch recess.

Holy shit. I was unprepared either way. There's no way to prepare for this, testifying on behalf of your father who is on trial for murdering your mother? What the fuck! You can't make this up. I knew I would be fine up there because I know how to tell the truth. I know my father and the kind of man he has been to me, but I don't think anything can prepare a person for a moment like this.

I was grateful for the recess. We gathered at Mike's Catfish for lunch. This would be our final lunch together as a group regardless of the outcome. These people would never be together at one table ever again. These lunches had become a lifeline for me. The range of emotions and the ups and downs of the week were frazzling, and these lunches were the only time I felt at ease.

Here we are. It's only me left. Then we will know. I looked around, studying each face at the table. Everyone was in good spirits. My dad did his best, but the fatigue was heavy on his face. He picked at his food, unable to stomach much. I don't recall eating a single bite. We wrapped up lunch and headed back to the courthouse. My stress and anxiety levels began to skyrocket the closer we got. As I walked into the building, my heart felt like it would explode.

You're alright. Just breathe, I reminded myself. *You know this feeling. You're going to be alright, Lil'*—I caught myself. My heart went from beating wildly to sinking deep within my stomach. I had been about to console that six-year-old boy inside of me. I was consoling Lil' Reggie.

Breathe.

All the Reggies needed me right now. I kept repeating, *you're alright. Just breathe.* In my mind, I pictured all the versions of me that had carried this weight for far too long. The six-year-old me, mourning the loss of my mother. The fifteen-year-old me, just beginning to find myself. The twenty-six-year-old me trying to make my place in the world. The thirty-five-year-old me beginning to feel success despite the weight of my past. And there was me, now, a vessel for all of us.

You're alright. Just breathe . . .

FINAL WITNESS

"The Defense calls its final witness, Reginald Reed Jr."

I rose slowly, adjusted my jacket, and walked to the witness stand. My head was throbbing, and my body felt numb, like a shell. I was surprised that I could walk. It felt more like floating than walking. I made it to the witness stand and steadied myself for a moment. The bailiff could tell I was struggling, and she gave me extra time before beginning the oath.

"Please raise your right hand."

As soon as I began to raise my hand I fell apart. All the stress and anxiety welled up and out in waves that I could not control. There was total silence around me as decades of sorrow burst forth for all to see. I wanted so badly to be strong or at least to appear strong, but my emotions had other plans.

I looked around. So many people were crying. For a moment, I began to feel shame. This feeling was quickly covered by even deeper sadness, trauma, grief, pain, and loss. Endless years of emotions. Seeing my father begin to cry as well broke me in two. I was shattered. The bailiff handed me tissues, and I continued with the oath through streaming tears.

"Do you solemnly swear to tell the truth, the whole truth, and nothing but the truth, so help you God?"

"I do."

I sat, grateful to no longer be forced to rely on my legs to hold me. My father's attorney allowed me time to gather myself before beginning. She asked me first about my relationship with my mother. I told the courtroom that I sadly did not remember much about my mother. I was too young when she was killed to remember much.

"One thing I do know from other people telling me over the years is that we were very close, and I was a 'momma's boy'," I told the courtroom.

My aunts were sobbing, and my father continued to wipe tears from his eyes with a handkerchief. I tried hard not to fall apart again, digging my fingernails into my palms as a distraction. *Do not cry. Be strong. Do. Not. Cry.*

"Is there anything else you can tell us about your relationship with your mother? Any memories?"

Tears were still falling. I couldn't answer her question. My memory failed me. I was failing her, failing my mother. Why couldn't I remember? I beat myself up on the inside.

"I wish I could remember more. God, how I wish I remembered more. I just can't. I'm so sorry," I said, broken.

"That's quite alright," the attorney assured me. "You were so young—only six years old. We don't expect you to remember everything." She continued. "What do you remember about that night, the night your mother never came home?"

"I remember playing Nintendo with my father in the living room, and I remember we both fell asleep on the couch, but not much more than that," I answered. "Again, I'm so sorry. I wish I could tell you more. I just can't remember. I'm not even sure I have a memory of anything else. Playing Nintendo and falling asleep—that's all I can remember."

"It's okay, let's talk about your father. What kind of relationship do you have with your father, Reggie?"

"I have a good relationship with my father. He did a great job raising me. He taught me everything I know, and he taught me how to navigate through life."

The sadness welled up inside of me again, uncontrollable. I began to sob. Through my tears, I managed to continue.

"My father is my rock. I wouldn't be the man I am today if it weren't for my father. He is everything to me."

"How do you feel sitting here today, testifying on behalf of your father?" the attorney asked.

"I feel very uneasy. I lost my mom, and now I'm up here, and I feel like I am about to lose my father, too."

There wasn't a dry eye in the courtroom, except for the prosecuting attorneys.

"No further questions, Your Honor."

The defense turned me over to the prosecution. I had no idea what to expect. I didn't know if they would grill me or take it easy on me. The defense had prepared me for either scenario. I dug my fingernails into my palms again. *Stay strong. Don't cry.*

The prosecutor stood up and walked slowly toward me with his head down. He didn't want to look at me. Maybe he felt guilty for having put me in this position. Maybe he wanted to appear as though he was sympathetic toward me. I stared him down until he finally made eye contact with me. I thought of all the things I wished I could say to him, out loud, for the whole courtroom to hear: *Damn you. Damn you for bringing this all back up in my life.*

Damn you for going after my father. Damn the deal you made with Jessie Lee Jones. Damn you.

"We aren't going to ask too many questions of you, Mr. Reed. There is one thing I'm curious about . . ."

Long pause. He's staring at the ground again. *I'm up here, you coward*, I thought.

"I saw you back there taking notes throughout the trial. Is all this information new to you? Have you not heard many of the pieces of evidence that have been presented here this week?"

He was trying to make it look like this was all new information to me, that I wasn't 100% wrapped up in this from the day it started. I knew everything, and he knew it.

"I'm just taking notes." I wasn't going to give him anything more than that.

"No further questions, Your Honor."

And that was it.

It felt like I was up there forever, but in reality, it was only about 25 minutes. I walked back to my seat, brushing my hand along my father's shoulder as I passed him. I hoped I had said enough; done enough. I wished there was more I could say and do. I was the final witness, and I felt the heaviness of that responsibility all the way to my core.

CLOSING STATEMENTS

Both the prosecution and defense gave their closing arguments after my testimony. The trial, lasting only a week, was much shorter than anyone expected. I braced myself for the prosecution's last opportunity to malign my father and paint him as a cold-blooded killer. Even so, I couldn't have prepared myself for what was coming.

The prosecution painted my father as an "evil mastermind." The inflection, tone, and volume of the attorney's voice preyed on the emotions of the jurors.

"Mr. Reed is an EVIL mastermind who orchestrated EVERY aspect of his wife's BRUTAL murder," he thundered.

The prosecutor forcefully pointed at my father and swung back, staring into the eyes of each of the twelve jurors, making sure to maintain eye contact with each as he flipped through images of the crime scene: My mother's clothes, the necklace clasp, and the life insurance policies. The jury was flooded with information, drama, and emotional tactics.

The attorney's voice was loud and aggressive, making everyone in the courtroom uncomfortable. I looked around. Some people's arms were crossed against their chests, some were staring down at the floor unable to watch, and many were rubbing their foreheads, trying to ease the stress of the situation. I felt cold, shivers running up and down my spine. I felt like I was hovering over the scene, a sort of out-of-body moment. I imagine that the jurors felt the intensity even more as he paced back and forth like an animal, staring into the jury box, his steely gaze lingering on each one in turn.

"Mr. Reed is an evil man! And Reggie Jr. is also a victim. If you want to prosecute THE DEVIL, you have to go to HELL to get your witnesses!"

I have no idea what this means. It makes no sense other than to confuse and incite an emotional response from the jury.

"Mr. Reed was so jealous of his wife and a rumored affair with a White man, and he COULD NOT—WOULD NOT live in the shadow of his wife. So, he concocted a PLAN. A plan to murder his wife in COLD BLOOD." He points angrily to the crime scene photo of my mother's body and continues. "He thought, *you want to be WHITE, I'll MAKE you White* and he smeared white fluid all over her dead body."

I felt sick, on the brink of throwing up or passing out. I braced myself against the wooden pew-like bench. My hands were sweating despite my body feeling ice-cold. I tried to keep notes, but my fine motor skills were completely shot. I couldn't move.

The prosecutor was unrelenting, playing every angle brought to trial against my father. He turned the lack of evidence against him at every turn. He was dead set on making the jury feel like my father was the literal devil.

"Mr. Reed PUNCTURED his wife seventeen—SEVENTEEN—times in the chest. He didn't just want her DEAD, he wanted her DESTROYED."

I considered getting up and walking out of the courtroom, but I was afraid my legs would betray me. This was all too loud;

too aggressive. It was too much. He was preying on everyone's emotions.

"SELONIA REED NEEDS YOU. The FAMILY of Selonia Reed NEEDS YOU. They need each and every one of YOU to bring justice for their dead sister." Then, he dropped the hammer with these words: "The DUTY of the LIVING is to bring JUSTICE for the DEAD!"

Holy shit.

My nerves were shot.

The courtroom was silent.

I prayed for it to all be over.

The defense attorney walked to the podium, took the microphone in hand, and walked back and forth in front of the jury box. She began explaining the charge against my father: Second-Degree Murder.

"Second-Degree Murder is NOT Conspiracy. Second-Degree Murder is NOT Collusion. Second-Degree Murder is NOT Solicitation. Second-Degree Murder is committing the crime of murder. To find Mr. Reed guilty of Second-Degree Murder you must believe WITHOUT A SHADOW OF DOUBT that Mr. Reed killed his wife, Selonia Reed. To find Mr. Reed guilty of Second-Degree Murder, you must believe WITHOUT A SHADOW OF DOUBT that the evidence presented in this case proves that Mr. Reed killed his wife. This is your DUTY as a jury. You must set aside all emotion and look only at the facts presented in this courtroom over the last four days to determine Mr. Reed's fate. You must be impartial, and unbiased." She pauses. "Do you believe the prosecution presented a perfect case, without flaw, so much so that all twelve of you can say without a shadow of doubt that Mr. Reed is guilty of killing his wife?" She surveyed the jurors, looking each one in the eye.

"Mr. Reed is NOT an evil mastermind. He was and still is a well-respected member of his community. He did right by his son and stayed put after his wife was brutally murdered. He was a good father. He raised a fine young man."

She ended with a final plea to the jury: "Do your duty."

And with that, the trial was over.

The judge gave the jury instructions, they filed out, and we all cleared the courtroom.

It was 4:02 p.m.

A QUESTION

After closing arguments, we all went to a local restaurant together. My uncles and aunts were there, Quentin and his brother, as well as the team of attorneys defending my father. We all had an opportunity to express the gratitude we all felt for the attorney who had represented my father. From the very beginning, she was on top of everything. She was always willing to engage with me when I knew she didn't have to, and she answered every question I had leading up to the trial.

When I say she fought hard for my father, that is a vast understatement.

She argued my father's case with every fiber of her being. She was dynamic, moving around the courtroom, pointing out every hole in the prosecution's case—and there were many. She fought for my father, but if I am being honest, I believe she was also fighting for *me*.

This is the mark of a great attorney.

We all felt confident that the defense had poked so many holes in the prosecution's case that we surely would have convinced at least one juror. That's all we needed—just one juror to believe he was not guilty, and we would have a hung jury and a mistrial. A mistrial is by definition the termination of a trial before its normal conclusion because of a procedural error; statements by a witness, judge, or attorney which prejudice a jury; a deadlock by a jury without reaching a verdict after lengthy deliberation (also known as a "hung" jury); or the failure to complete a trial within the time set by the court. In situations such as this the judge, either on his own initiative or upon the request of one of the parties, will declare a mistrial, dismiss the jury, and direct that the prosecution be set for trial again, starting from the very beginning. This is what we needed.

We ordered food and talked over the details of the trial. Everyone seemed confident that it would go in our favor. I sat back and observed mostly, knowing that at the end of the day, every single one of us would have the opportunity to go back to the safety of our homes and the comfort of our loved ones. That may not happen for my father. This whole thing could go sideways. I wasn't ready to celebrate anything until the final verdict had been read.

At 5:06 p.m. a question was brought over from the jury. Just over one hour in, the jury was seeking clarification on the difference between Second-Degree Murder and Manslaughter. The attorneys and my father gathered their things and headed back to the courthouse. The rest of us stayed behind for just a few more minutes before heading back to the public defender's office.

At 5:40 p.m. the jury sent an offer: Thirty years for a guilty plea. My father denied the offer.

Tensions were high and the conversations were quickly going silent. I was sitting next to my father who leaned back in his chair, exhausted. As exhausted and beaten down as he was, he was not going to admit to a crime he did not commit, even if that meant risking life in prison.

At 7:13 p.m. we got the call that the verdict was in.

The jury deliberated the fate of my father for just 3 hours and 11 minutes. *Fuck.*

We made the walk back to the courthouse. It was dark now, and bitterly cold. I could see the prosecuting team as they walked. They seemed to have a swagger in their steps. My heart rate went through the roof, and my head throbbed. I was in complete panic mode. The courthouse was surrounded by police vehicles with their blue lights illuminated. It was surreal. My dad and I walked side by side.

Why are all these police here?

Why do they have their lights turned on?

Shit, shit, shit.

We went through the metal detectors on the first floor and were wanded down by security with hand-held metal detectors before entering the courtroom. *This doesn't feel normal. This is really about to go down. How the hell did we get here? How in the actual hell did we get here?* The past three years flashed in my mind, and I would have made a deal with the devil himself at that moment if I could just go back. My mind was racing, made worse when I saw that the courtroom was filled with heavily armed SWAT.

I took my seat but could not be still. I felt like I was about to jump out of my skin. My fight-or-flight response was in full swing, and I had to fight hard to stay put and not run. I leaned over to the victim's advocate and asked her if this was normal. She tried hard to reassure me that everything happening was very normal, but I could tell she was lying to me. She was just trying to be kind. It was freezing and my whole body was shaking, I bobbed one leg up and down to keep from going completely numb.

The judge entered and we all stood. The jury walked in a single-file line, stopping to stand in front of each of their chairs. The foreman handed the verdict to the judge. He read it silently, then handed it to his secretary to be read aloud. As she began, I could hear a slight quiver in her voice.

No! No! No! No! No! No! I was screaming on the inside.

"On this day, the 18th of November 2022, in the twenty-first District Court of Amite City, Louisiana, we, the jury, find the defendant Reginald Reed Senior . . . "

GUILTY

———

"**G**uilty of Second-Degree Murder."

. . .   *Don't lock your knees, don't lock your knees.*

I was in shock. My whole body felt like it had been electrified, every hair on my body standing on end. I wanted to cry, but no tears would come. I knew all along that this entire situation could go sideways, but I had always held out hope that everything would be okay.

They got it wrong. They got it wrong. I wanted to scream at the jurors. *You got it wrong! You did NOT do your duty! The prosecution did not prove without a shadow of a doubt that my father killed my mother! What is wrong with you? You got it all wrong!*

"Mr. Reed, you have been found guilty of the Second-Degree Murder of Selonia Reed. This verdict carries a sentence of mandatory life in prison without the possibility of probation or parole."

My father would spend the rest of his life in prison. He would die there—alone.

I expected there to be more reaction from my mother's side of the family, but everyone was silent, feeling the same shock that I was feeling. The judge said a few words that I can't recall, dismissed the jury, and brought the case to a close with one crack of the wooden gavel against the bench. The sound broke my shock. I was looking around, desperately trying to make sense of what had just happened. I landed on the face of the defense attorney.

"Do you want to come say goodbye to your dad, Reggie?" she asked me.

As I approached my father, he began emptying his pockets. He laid down his phone, house keys, and wallet. He took off his watch and pulled out a small white handkerchief from the inside pocket of his jacket. He handed the handkerchief to me. I could feel that there was something wrapped up inside, but I couldn't bear to open it just then.

My father grabbed me up into a big hug. I wanted to stay there forever.

"Everything's gonna be alright. Stay strong. I'll stay strong, and you stay strong too, okay?"

He pulled back for a moment, looked me in the eyes, and kissed me on the forehead. We embraced once more, and then they took him away from me.

I melted down.

The cries that came out of my body were guttural—primal.

From the depths I wailed; "I want my daddy. I want my daddy. I want my daddy."

Here he was, that little boy from the interrogation videos who just wanted his daddy. The tone of my voice resembled that of my six-year-old self, high-pitched and desperate to be in the comfort of my father's presence. My uncles and aunts gathered around me but nothing or no one could have comforted me in that moment, only my father.

And they took him away from me.

The attorneys tried to be strong and positive, saying something to me about an appeal. I just nodded my head. I had no more words. I felt beaten. I walked out of the courthouse in a haze. It was darker and more frigid than it had been just 20 minutes prior. The air felt heavy, and I felt weak against it.

I finally made it to my car and looked over at the empty passenger seat. I could still smell my father's cologne and felt a mixture of comfort and deep despair. I pulled out my phone but forgot how it worked for a moment. My fingers were frozen and stiff. I numbly punched in my passcode and called my wife, Paula. She picked up on the first ring, and I uttered just one word: "Guilty." She broke down and we sat there together, crying, unable to form words.

I reached into my pocket and pulled out the folded handkerchief my father had handed me. It smelled like him. I held it to my nose and inhaled deeply before unwrapping it. Inside was a small delicate rosary made up of tiny pearl-like beads. I ran my fingers along them thinking of the many prayers my father must have prayed over the last 35 years. *He must have prayed for me*, I thought.

Now, I will pray for him.

BIBLE

I drove over to my childhood home on Apple Street the day after the verdict was delivered. I had done the same thing just twenty-four hours ago, only then my father had been there, waiting on the tiny porch in his suit and tie. The sky had been crisp and blue, and the birds were chirping. Today, everything was overcast and grey. A mist hung in the air and the entire world felt silent.

The house looked different, too; older, and more worn down. I sat staring at it for a long time before exiting the car and going inside. My secret hope was that my father had left something for me, a letter or something to help me make sense of the last week; hell, the last 35 years. The house was in good order. The dishes had been washed and laid to dry on a faded blue towel. The blinds were pulled up, and the curtains were open. My father's bed was made, his pajamas folded at the foot of it. His toothbrush and razor lay neatly, side by side, next to the bathroom sink.

Everything looked as if my father had been fully expecting to return home.

I noticed his Bible sitting on the living room table. The cover was marked by years of use, its black leather felt like dry cracked earth. Yellow and blue post-it notes stuck out everywhere. *Places my father marked*, I thought. For a moment, I considered that I shouldn't look inside. This was his Bible. *Wouldn't that be an*

invasion of privacy? In the end, my longing to find something—
anything—from him, won.

I opened the Bible, and my father's familiar scent rose from
its pages.

The Bible seemed to naturally fall open to the book of Isaiah.
Many of the scriptures were marked with stars and asterisks in
either black or blue ink. I recognized my father's handwriting
in the margins. There was a freshly drawn circle around Isaiah
49.10: "They shall not hunger nor thirst; neither shall the heat
nor sun smite them: for he that hath mercy on them shall lead
them, even by the springs of water he shall guide them." Below
the scripture was a note written by my father:

*Lord Jesus, I pray you keep me free. I love you Lord because you have
heard my voice and my supplication, Amen.*

On this same page, he had written a list of names: Emily, Joe,
Reggie, Lathan, Paula, and Laurene.

Next to each name was a time: 2:47, 2:52, 2:58, 3:10, 3:15,
3:17,

It dawned on me that this was a list of people for whom he
had prayed, and he had listed the time in which he had done
so beside each name. I wondered if this was a daily prayer list,
perhaps a routine he had established. But who were Emily, Joe,
and Laurene? I knew my father was a religious man, but I had
no idea his relationship with prayer and scripture was this deep.
Knowing it brought me comfort. I turned to the next post-it,

this one in Ephesians. There I found a handwritten list entitled "God's Plans for Me!"

God promises to watch over your life!
God plans to support and bless you.
God plans for peace, love, and everything else!
God has good things in store for you . . . that good is coming your way.
Get ready: Your time is coming. God is doing a new thing!
You may be in a dry place, but you aren't going to stay there. Renewal is coming. Favor is coming.
Healing is coming. Breakthrough is coming. God can do it all!
The new thing is not going to be ordinary. It's going to catapult you ahead. God is going to take you higher than ever before.

I have no idea when this was written, but I couldn't help but wonder if this was my father's way of preparing for and getting through the week of the trial. Everything about the Bible and his handwritten notes led me to believe that he had leaned heavily on God for an exceedingly long time. I knew that he would have never shown me this part of himself. I think he might have even worried that I would perceive it as a weakness. He always wanted me to see him as a strong man, and it brought me some peace to see he had been able to be weak with God; to rely on Him and His promises.

I sank back into the old couch. It was the same couch my father and I had sat on playing Nintendo the night my mother never came home. My mind flooded with images—were these memories? I could see my mother standing in front of the small mirror near the front door, her brown hands smoothing out her black T-shirt and jeans before turning to hug and kiss me good-bye. I could see—and feel—my father sitting beside me on the couch, laughing and cheering me on as we played Super Mario Brothers. I could smell pepperoni pizza cooking in the oven.

If only I could go back to that night. If I could go back, I would keep her *here*, safe, with us. I would have demanded that my mother stay home. I would have played sick because I know she would have never left if she thought I was ill. I imagine it: She comes to kiss me goodbye, and I say, "Mommy, I don't feel good."

"What's the matter, son?" she says putting her soft hand on my small forehead. "You don't have a fever."

"It's my stomach," I lie.

"Okay, I'll get you some 7-UP. That'll settle your stomach." She walks over to the phone, and I hear her dialing.

"Hi, it's me, Selonia . . . listen, I'm not gonna be able to go out tonight. Lil' Reggie isn't feeling good. Alright, I will . . . talk to you later."

She hangs up and goes to the kitchen to pour me a glass of 7-Up, then returns to join me and my dad on the couch. It's a tight fit but being close to her is all I want. She grabs a Nintendo controller from the table and says, "What are we playing tonight?" My father responds, smiling, "Whatever Lil' Reggie wants."

I look at them on both sides of me. My mother, *and* my father, and I smile so big my face hurts.

I've done it.

I've saved my mother.

I've saved my father.

I've saved my family.

I stayed there on the old couch, dreaming this dream. I didn't want to leave the scenario I had imagined or accept that history had not changed. Perhaps even the tiniest fluctuation in the timeline would have stopped it from happening at all, and been the catalyst to put it all right for me, my mother, my father—for my family. I could have grown up with my mother and father. I could have had an entirely different life. My mother could have known my son—her grandson. My parents could have lived out their days together in this house on Apple Street. My father could have taught Lathan how to swing a bat and catch a baseball, and my mother could have taught Paula how to cook her famous fried fish.

We could have been a family. We would have spent holidays and birthdays together laughing and enjoying one another's company. We could have been so happy. Everything could have been so different if just *one* thing would have been different. Reality flashed before me, and I recalled the holidays and birthdays spent with just me and my dad. My mother's birthday, Mother's Day, anniversaries, even the day she didn't come home. I recalled *feeling* her absence and longing for a mother.

My dream state began to take a turn as anger and regret washed over me. As the fog began to clear I realized I was clutching the Bible with both hands, my knuckles white and numb.

Why did she have to go out that night? Why?

WHERE'S DADDY

The drive back to San Antonio was long and the weather was terrible, with a mix of heavy rain and storms the entire way. I was anxious to be home but forced to take my time. As I drove, I replayed the events of the trip in my head: Waking up the first morning of trial feeling like I was stuck in a nightmare; picking my father up each morning, the smell of his cologne, our trips to McDonald's, and our small talk on the drive to Amite City. I reviewed the jury selection, opening statements, and the faces of each witness. I smiled remembering our lunches together with family and gripped the steering wheel as I played and replayed the evidence, my testimony, and closing arguments. I wanted to fast forward through the verdict, watching myself as I clutched my father and cried like a six-year-old boy.

I lingered a while in my childhood home, seeing the worn Bible in my hand, watching as I lay my head back on the weathered couch cushions and dreamed a dream of saving my family.

So much had happened in the space of just one week. We had waited so long to finally get to the trial, and now it felt like it was all over in the blink of an eye. The permanence struck me: It is what it is now, and there was no way for me or anyone else to change any of it. My mother was still gone, and I had no more clarity about her murder than I did going into the trial. No closure, and still so many questions remained unanswered.

There was still so much that didn't add up for me. *Could we have fought harder for a more diverse jury? If we had a different set of people, could there have been a completely different outcome? Should the defense attorney's opening statements have sought to prey on the jury's emotions, like the prosecution did?*

The evidence—my mother's belongings and her soiled clothing—could have sunk us from the very start. Seeing those things up close may have been the one thing that solidified the minds of the jury. I kept coming back to the prosecution. They so desperately wanted my father. They were going to say and do anything to get him, even if it wasn't the truth.

Dammit. Dammit dammit.

I beat myself up over everything. *We should have done _____. We could have done _____. We shouldn't have _____.* I kept coming back to Jessie Lee Jones and the young man who testified about information Jones had shared with him in prison. Anger bubbled up inside of me. *Jessie Lee Jones is a fucking free man. He described killing my mother in detail, with his brother, and he is fucking free while my father will die in prison.* We should have done more with this information. Why couldn't we have done *more?*

The mental ping-pong continued throughout the entire drive home. It was after midnight when I pulled into my driveway. Everyone was asleep. Rather than wake Paula, I went to the spare bedroom and got into bed, pulling the cool sheets up to my chin. I was exhausted and fell instantly into a deep sleep.

I woke to the sound of my son Lathan's little voice. "Mommy, where's daddy? Where's daddy, mommy?"

I wanted so badly to just lie there, pull the covers up over my head, and disappear. Life felt unlivable. Everything felt too hard and too heavy. So many times throughout the process I considered the fact that *I* could just give up, let everything get the best of me, and pull me under. It would be *easier* to quit. It would be *easier* to stop living. There were so many times that I thought, *just fuck it*; but something within me always pulled me back.

"Mommy, where's daddy?" Today the force pulling me back was my son. I had to go on, for him. I had to get up, get dressed, put on a strong face, and show up for him despite how miserable I felt. This is what it means to be a father. I have a whole new understanding and respect for my father now. He had to *choose* to keep living after my mother was so violently taken from us. He woke up every morning, got dressed, put on a brave face, and continued living—every day—for me.

I walked into the kitchen and Lathan screamed, "Daddy! Daddy! Daddy!" his little arms outstretched, reaching for me. I scooped him up in my arms and hugged him harder than I ever had before.

For him—*because* of him—I will never give up.

PANIC ATTACKS

My heart has begun beating double time since the trial. My brain has valiantly borne the weight of the stress, but my body is throwing up red flags. The culmination of everything weighs so heavily on me. During the day when I'm busy with work or spending time with Paula and Lathan, I am fine. It's the quiet time that gets me. When everyone has gone to sleep, the anxiety comes like an uncontrollable wave swelling in my chest. The visceral nature of it can't be ignored. I can literally feel the stress grinding like gears within my body. During these times I would do anything to shed my skin; to not feel anything.

If I were a drinker, I would drink. If I were a pill popper, I would pop pills. If I were anyone other than me, I would do anything and everything I could to escape my own body. But I don't know how to escape. I'm stuck with myself and the fallout of the past three decades. I try to trick myself into believing that *it's nothing. I'm fine. My heart rate is just fast. It's not a big deal.* This works a lot of the time—until it doesn't.

The body keeps the score, as they say.

I realize the holidays are making everything feel heavier. Holidays are always hard, but this is my first Thanksgiving, Christmas, and birthday without my mother *or* my father. The stress of the trial lingers, and I find that I am forcing myself to be part of the festivities. Honestly, I'd rather just be alone.

The new year brought some relief; it is a *new* year, after all. The holidays are behind me, and I can feel myself slowly but surely regaining some strength. I still have bad days here and there, but I am beginning to experience some good days, too.

I relish the good days.

On the good days, I feel in control of my circumstances and emotions. I can look at my situation and say that although things have been grueling, I have made it through. I feel as though I am regaining resilience and building strength in new areas, many of which I hadn't previously experienced. But, such is life. All I can do now is let the days come and go and hope that in time the good days will start to outnumber the bad. It's a waiting game. Again, more waiting.

DEAR DAD

They tell me you are being transferred to a prison outside of Baton Rouge, but I have not heard from you and have been unable to reach you for weeks. The last time we saw each other on the video call from the Tangipahoa Parish Jail your face was battered—dried blood, bruises and your right eye was completely black and swollen. You didn't mention it, so I didn't either. I am worried. I know when you enter jail or prison as a new inmate there is a hazing of sorts, and I wonder what could have happened for someone to beat you like this. There has been so much chatter on social media and apparently the rumor mill in Hammond is in full swing. Quentin has kept me updated daily.

The detective who reopened the case against you reached out and has told me he is willing to walk me through each and every detail of the evidence. He is sure that you are 100% guilty. Why is he so sure? What does he know? What evidence does he have? He tells me that if we do speak, it must be in person and that I should make sure to bring Paula because I will be shocked by what I hear. He alludes to me having been present during the crime—what? I was only six—how could I have been there? Why was I there? This makes no sense. Did I see my mother get murdered or hear her *being* murdered? He says you had help from one of our family members. Is this true? He speaks with such authority which makes me question *everything*.

I don't know whether I should meet with him. I don't know whether I believe him. I don't know what his motive is—the case being over and done. Rumors of your involvement run rampant in Hammond. People talk openly—no longer in hushed conversations—about how they always "knew it was you." They say that you finally got what was coming. They talk about you the way the prosecution did, saying you're "an evil mastermind." They borrow headlines and social media chatter and make it their own. They say they feel safer now that the *cold case* has been solved. People praise the prosecution for finally bringing justice for my mother and her family. I guess that includes me, but that feels so strange. You being in prison for the rest of your life with your face bloody and battered feels far from justice to me.

I'm still heartbroken, and confused, and can't pinpoint where everything went sideways. I run the details of the trial in my mind in an endless loop. I have been struggling with anxiety and have had a few significant panic attacks. I even ended up in the emergency room once. My heart races constantly. It's my new normal. I find myself trying to stay busy to keep my thoughts at bay, but I know that's not sustainable.

This part of my story feels terrible. I feel helpless. I still had hope going into the trial, but that hope is gone. The defense talks of an appeal; but if I am being honest, I don't think that will ever happen. I worry I will feel this way forever, though Paula assures me it's going to get better with time. I feel like I have been waiting on "time" all my life. When do I get to go on? Move forward? Put this all behind me? I don't see that ever happening and that makes me feel like I can't breathe. I don't want to live my life this way. I did nothing to deserve it. I wish my story were different.

Parts of my natural curiosity about my mother's murder have surfaced now that the dust has settled. I wonder about the car-wash witness and her testimony that she saw you there that night. Did she really see you? Why would she lie? She was able to pick you out of a photo lineup. If she saw you, where was I? Apparently, I was not at my grandmother's. Where was I? If she's being honest, why were you at the carwash that night? You have always reinforced my memory that we were at home together playing Nintendo until we both fell asleep. Did you leave the house after I fell asleep? Why did you take out so many life insur-ance policies on my mother? She was young and healthy. Who needs that much life insurance at 26 years old? And the timing— why did you take out so many policies in such close proximity to her murder?

These facts trouble me and make me question.

I've never spoken to you about this, and I wonder what your motivation was. In hindsight, I can see how this may have been a sticking point for the jury. It's a red flag for sure, and I'm hoping someday you can explain this to me. I'm still hung up on Jessie Lee Jones and the deal he struck with the prosecution. They traded him his freedom to get to you. It seems so unfair. They turned him against you. He is free and you will die in prison.

I am angry.

Why didn't your defense team do more with the tip from the young man in prison? Is there something else we could have done differently, or were the events always going to play out this way, with Jones just a pawn in their game to get you? I wonder if we should have had you testify. I wonder what the defense could have asked you that would have shown the jury who you really are and let them see that you were a man from a well-respected family, that you did stay with me after an incredible loss, and that despite it all you were a very good father to me. But then I think of the prosecution and how they would have tried to destroy you. One moment I feel like we should have taken the risk, and then the next I am sure we made the right choice. I don't know. I will never know. It doesn't matter now. The "what if we would have" and "we should haves" are unsettling and exhausting.

I think about the jury a lot. I can clearly picture each of their faces and even remember their demeanors. I long to know what they were thinking throughout the trial. What did they talk about behind closed doors? Did they take their duty seriously? They only deliberated for 3 hours and 11 minutes. How could they have been so sure you were guilty? Two young Black female jurors seemed sympathetic to our case the entire trial. I wonder if the more senior members of the jury ran roughshod over them, and they acquiesced to the group. I think that happens with juries, though it's not supposed to be that way.

I hope one day we will be able to sit down and talk—really talk—and I can ask you all the lingering questions I have. I hope you will be totally honest with me. I think I deserve to know the whole truth. Like, why didn't you do more after my mother was killed? If my wife were murdered, I would never stop trying to find out who did it. I would knock on doors, hang up signs, make phone calls . . . I would do ANYTHING to find the killer. I wouldn't ever stop. Did you try? Did you do everything you could?

Please don't think this means I don't love you. That will never change, no matter what you tell me. You will always be my hero and my rock. I will always love you no matter what. People don't just stop loving people. I can promise you that if we ever have the opportunity to discuss all my questions, nothing you say will change our relationship. I have been by your side and have supported you for the last three years and I will keep doing so forever.

Is there anything you know that I don't know?

Would you be willing to answer all my questions?

Can we talk openly and with total honesty about what happened?

I'm not naïve. You must know more than you've told me. I need to hear the truth. I feel I deserve to know the truth. I don't even know if I will send you this letter. I worry it would be hurtful to you, but I don't know what to do with all the questions.

I need closure.

Your son,

Lil' Reggie

YOU HAVE A COLLECT CALL

It hits me out of nowhere. I'll just be going about my day and the call comes.

"You have a collect call from Tangipahoa Parish Prison. Press one to accept."

My stomach sinks, but I press one. I will never *not* press one. I don't care where I am or what I am doing, I will always press one.

I have to.

Here's where it gets tricky. I am always happy to hear from him, of course, but in many ways these calls keep me locked in trauma. It's like my father died in November. I lost him. I grieved his loss like I would a death. I went through all the stages of grief:

Denial—Just don't think about it. Kick the can. Keep it moving.

Anger—What the fuck?! The jury got it wrong. Jessie Lee Jones is free—he's even committed another crime since he has been out—but my father is locked up for life?

Bargaining—Thinking through the what-ifs of an appeal and obsessing about the trial and the details that may have swung things against us.

Depression—I could just give up and say *what the hell* to it all. Throw my hands up and succumb.

Acceptance—I am beginning to regain myself. This is just another piece of my story.

Some days I cycle through all the stages. I may wake up angry, but by the end of the day when I am putting Lathan to bed, all feels good with the world, and I feel acceptance. The next day I might wake up bargaining, playing everything over and over in my mind. I may stay locked in this stage most of the day. The exhaustion of the mental game can make me feel depleted, which is my version of depression. I go inward and isolate myself to try and numb it.

My feelings can change on a dime. It's a fucking roller coaster. No one else knows, though. I keep it all concealed. From the outside, it's all good. I'm good. Honestly, I don't know how *not* to look strong. I legitimately don't know how to completely fall apart. It's not in my make-up, which I have learned is both a blessing and a curse.

Back to the tricky part.

I get these phone calls. They're like an electric shock; like I'm some sort of lab rat, doing fine, running all the mazes, and doing all the things, and then . . . BAM. The phone rings. Unknown Number. I know what's coming next.

"You have a collect call . . . " I want to talk to him. I want to know that he's okay.

I also desperately want my life to go on.

The constant reminder of his situation—his life in prison—is unbearable at times. There is nothing I can do to get him out of there. Talking to him on the phone is like rubbing salt in a raw wound, but I have no choice. What's the alternative? Ignore him? Never.

The things he shares with me make me feel helpless and awful. He hasn't eaten anything but a bologna sandwich in days. It's 110 degrees and there's no air conditioning. He must wash his clothes in the toilet. They shaved his head. What am I supposed to do with this information? I can't do a single thing to change it, so I just have to feel it and carry it around with me.

More weight.

I don't want to carry this any longer, but I would never and will never turn my back on my father.

I will always press one.

TIME

It has been almost 11 months since the trial. The sting is less powerful. I have good days, and I have bad days. On the bad days, I find myself ruminating, obsessing over the details, and thinking about how things could have turned out differently—for everyone. The bad days are exhausting. My mind never stops. I have no idea what brings this on, and I have yet to figure out how to stop it. I just let it happen and hope the next day will be a good one.

On a good day, I am busy, and the thoughts don't have space or time to surface. They are still there, but they're not as loud or overwhelming. On a good day, I feel more in control of my thoughts and emotions. My heart still races a lot, but the panic attacks have stopped. I am busier at work than I have ever been, which feels like a blessing. Lathan is getting so big, and we are beginning to see his personality developing. He loves his mother and I think he thinks I'm pretty alright, too.

Paula is thriving in her career, and it brings me so much joy to see her doing something she loves and is so incredibly talented at. We have decided to move to a larger space and are building a house with a big back yard for Lathan.

I talk to Quentin almost every day. His unfailing friendship has been a lifeline for me. I can never thank him enough for the constant support he has given me and my father over the last three years. Quentin is the kind of best friend I wish everyone had.

Writing this book has been such a source of healing for me. I have poured my heart out in these pages. The countless hours spent pecking away at the keyboard have brought much-needed catharsis, something that I desperately needed. I don't think I would be where I am today if I hadn't used writing as a means to process my story. There were many days I thought I would give up, but as is the case for much of my life something kept drawing me back in to do the work—to finish strong.

I feel stronger today than I did three months ago and know that in three more months, I'll be even stronger. It's funny how time does that. You never believe it when someone says, "Give it time," but it's the truth. I don't believe time heals all wounds, but time does allow for a greater perspective, and with perspective we can begin to make sense of the things we've been through.

I hope this book finds its way into the hands of people who are trying to heal. I hope my story will be of some comfort to those who are hurting or feel trapped in impossible circumstances. If I can help just one person make sense of their struggles and come out stronger on the other side, I will consider this journey a major success.

Love your people. Spend time with your family. Tell people you love them. Say the words "I love you." Look people in the eyes. Be kind. Be compassionate. Be generous with your time, energy, and resources. Take walks. Play catch with your kids. Take the vacation; work will be there when you return. Take pictures. Smile. Laugh. Hold hands. Hug people, encourage them, be a good friend, and learn to love yourself through the challenging times.

It will get easier, I promise.

I will always miss my mother. I will always have questions, but I have come to a place of acceptance. If I am to have closure, I trust that it will come when and how it is supposed to. I feel my mother is at peace, and that brings me deep comfort.

I will never get over my father being locked up behind bars. I will never stop loving him. If an appeal does happen, I will never stop fighting for him. I will tell Lathan about him and what a great father he was. His absence hurts, but I can't live my life in a place of hurt any longer; I know he wouldn't want me to.

Despite everything, I feel hope and I feel loved. I have many moments of deep peace and know that with time, many more will come. I have learned to be patient with myself and the myriad feelings that come and go. I have worked through the regret, and I am not angry.

I love the life I have built with Paula. This life is more than I could have ever imagined for myself. I feel proud of how far I've come, and I look forward to what the future holds.

My trauma will always be a part of who I am. I can't go back in time and change the past. I can't change what I have lived through. There will always be wounds and scars, and while I may need to tend to them for the rest of my life, they do not define me.

I feel differently than I did at the start of this process. I feel sure of myself. I trust myself. I have been to the depths, and I found my way back to the surface. I can honestly say, I feel like

I have become a stronger and more resilient man. I am certain I did everything I could, and I did so with honesty and integrity, never changing the person I am.

No more kicking the can; those days are over. There is too much life to live, and I refuse to exist on autopilot. I want to be present, active, and aware in my life.

No more kicking the can.

My head is up.

Eyes forward.

Shoulders back.

Moving on.

NEW LIFE

S o much has been taken from me.
My mother.
My father.

The magnitude of loss is overwhelming. And these are just the tangible things, that ones that people can see and understand. There is so much more loss within me that even I can't wrap my head around the sum of it. Writing this book has been cathartic and restorative in many ways, yet there are still places deep inside that will take more time and more tending to heal. I can't change the facts. My mother is gone, and now my father is as well. The weight of these facts threatens to pull me under, but I am and always will be a fighter.

Part of me has had to set aside this story and call it the past. I can't live within it any longer. That doesn't mean I don't care, or that it doesn't affect me. It simply means that I have learned that I need to build strong boundaries around myself and my life moving forward. I don't want this to be my only story. I don't want pain, loss, tragedy, and trauma to define me.

I am so much more. I deserve so much more. My family needs *all* of me; needs me to be alive and present with them now and in our future together. My son deserves a father who isn't preoccupied with the past and my wife deserves a husband who is fulling present on our marriage. My family deserves to write a new story.

I am ready for my life to be restored and to be on the receiving end of good things for once. I am craving positive energy and newness. I am done with my old ways of thinking and doing and am eager to move forward with a new perspective, willing to learn new ways of *actually* living rather than just surviving. After the trial, Paula and I decided we wanted to try to have another baby. We didn't want Lathan to grow up as an only child. We wanted something *good* to look forward to after so much pain, loss, and heartache.

We weren't sure how things would go. We are both older now, and we knew it could take time and possibly even medical intervention to become pregnant. We were acutely aware of the possibility of more loss, but we were both excited and ready to try. Nothing happened at first, and we quickly became discouraged. Some of my old thinking patterns began to creep in and I had to consciously fight back feelings of failure. We got to a place where we believed that this wasn't the path for us, that perhaps we were meant to be parents to an only child.

We made peace with this path.

But God had other plans. He was preparing us in His own time for the joy that was to come. Paula woke me in the early morning hours, pregnancy test in hand. She was smiling ear to ear, and I could tell she had been crying. She waved the little stick in front of my face as I reached up to steady her hand and get a good look at the results. The bright pink plus sign felt like a miracle.

"You're pregnant?" I asked, knowing the answer but needing her reassurance.

"Yes!" she said through streaming tears. "It's really early and anything could happen, but YES!"

We lay there together, just staring at the test. Neither of us could believe what we were seeing. We had all the feelings—fear, joy, disbelief, worry, what ifs. We held our breath the first few months and told only a few people the news, afraid of what could happen. As each appointment went well and the baby continued to grow, we began allowing ourselves to get more and more excited. We debated whether it would be a boy or a girl. Not that it mattered to either of us. A healthy baby is all we care about. We had the doctor write the gender on a slip of paper and put it in an envelope. We made cake pops and hosted a small gender reveal party, just me, Paula, and Lathan. Our little family is about to grow.

Lathan's excitement was priceless. As we all bit into the pops Lathan saw the bright pink cake inside and exclaimed, "Pink! I'm gonna have a baby sister!" It was a moment of pure joy. New life. New beginnings. A baby girl. A sister. A daughter. We are already so in love with her. Without discussion, Paula and I knew what we would name her. It is the only name, the *perfect* name.

Her name will be Selonia.

ACKNOWLEDGMENTS

I would like to acknowledge the immense support and love that has shaped my journey and express my deepest gratitude to those who have played a significant role in the creation of my memoir.

First and foremost, I want to acknowledge God, whose presence and guidance have been the cornerstone of my life. Your blessings have provided me the strength, courage, and clarity that I needed to embark on this remarkable endeavor.

My beloved wife. Your unconditional love and constant belief in me have been my biggest sources of inspiration. You have been my anchor in times of doubt, always encouraging me to pursue my dreams. Your steadfast support and constant presence have meant the world to me.

Lastly—but certainly not least—my incredible son. Your innocent laughter, infectious joy, and unconditional love have brought so much light into my life. You have taught me the true meaning of resilience and perseverance, and I am forever grateful for the lessons you have unknowingly imparted upon me.

I would also like to thank my team and editor for their belief in this project. Your guidance, feedback, and commitment to excellence have helped shape this memoir into its final form. Your dedication to amplifying my story is sincerely valued.

This journey of writing a true crime memoir has been emotionally challenging and intellectually stimulating. It is through the collective efforts and generosity of those mentioned above that this book has come to fruition. Without the love, support, and understanding of these remarkable individuals, this memoir would not have been possible. I am humbled by their presence in my life and eternally grateful for their support.

ABOUT THE AUTHOR

Reginald L. Reed Jr. is an author and an accomplished professional in the Pharmaceutical industry. He holds a Master's Degree in Business and Global Marketing. In his first book, *The Day My Mother Never Came Home*, Reed recalls the events surrounding the unsolved murder of his mother and the subsequent indictment and trial of his father, 32 years later. Reginald resides in San Antonio Texas with his wife Paula, their son Lathan and daughter Selonia.

Learn more about Reggie at www.rlreed.com.

Printed in Great Britain
by Amazon

44488652R00169